# Dealing With Deities

# Dealing With Deities

## Practical Polytheistic Theology

### Raven Kaldera

Hubbardston, Massachusetts

**Asphodel Press**
12 Simond Hill Road
Hubbardston, MA 01452

Dealing With Deities: Practical Polytheistic Theology
© 2012 by Raven Kaldera
ISBN 978-1-938197-02-4

All rights reserved. Unless otherwise specified,
no part of this book may be reproduced in any form
or by any means without the permission of the author.

Printed in cooperation with
Lulu Enterprises, Inc.
860 Aviation Parkway, Suite 300
Morrisville, NC 27560

*To all the Gods and spirits that comfort, sustain, inspire, and put up with me and my many flaws.*

*To all my human loved ones who do the same, and especially to the ones who believe in me, and in my work.*

*In addition, I am indebted to the other thoughtful polytheistic Pagans with whom I have exchanged ideas on this subject. Even when we did not agree with each other, I learned crucial things about my own truths. When we did agree, or when they showed me a piece of the puzzle I had not seen before, they gave me a gift beyond price. Thank you, all of you mortals who helped me to develop my theology through glimpses of your own, and may you continue to bravely explore and discuss these controversial questions in the future.*

# Contents

Introduction: The Uncharted Wilderness of Pagan Theology .....7
Polytheism And Her Sisters: Defining Belief ..............................7
The Nature Of Deities..................................................................16
Worshiping Our Gods..................................................................27
What You Call Is What You Get: Aspects of the Divine ..........32
Going Higher: Immanence and Transcendence .......................43
Not Quite Divine: Spirits, Ancestors, and Animism ..................49
Being In Relationship: The Human-Divine Exchange................55
Searching For Gods ....................................................................67
Pantheon Protocols .....................................................................71
The Search For Morality and Other Complications ...................80
Sacrifice, Smiting, and Silence: The Hard Parts Of
    Divine Relationship .................................................................85
Living In Mythic Time.................................................................97
Gender, Sex, and Gods...............................................................106
Death and Her Options ..............................................................110
Divination: Knowing What Is Knowable ..................................114
Epilogue: Living In the World, Honoring The Worlds ...........118
About The Author .......................................................................127

# Introduction:
# The Uncharted Wilderness of Pagan Theology

A Pagan friend of mine told me the tale: she was meeting a new person for a date, someone intelligent, thoughtful, and politically progressive. Someone not mired in the bigotries of conservative mainstream religions, someone whom she hoped would share her world view enough not to call her a devil-worshiper. Inevitably, the question of religion came up, and she told him that she was Pagan. He had heard of, and had even read some things about, her faith. However, his response to her was: "I'm surprised. You seem like such an intelligent and thoughtful person."

To him, Paganism wasn't a hive of evil demon-worship, which is what I hear most Pagans going on about when they talk about people thinking less of their religion. It was a childish, clumsy, unsophisticated practice that it didn't pay to look too hard at; a feel-good faith that was half unquestioned juvenile superstition and half rock-concert ecstasy. One might not even consider it a "faith" at all so much as a subculture, with more emphasis put on cultural activities than on any kind of real worship. It certainly wasn't a religion for mature and thoughtful adults who wanted to wrestle with tough spiritual questions within their religious framework.

This view of my faith is one that I'm increasingly coming up against within interfaith circles, and most modern Pagans that I've spoken to have few answers as to how to fix the problem. The few that do have answers tend to start with changing the subculture to be more palatable to other religious subcultures, which I believe is missing the point. The fact that we are fixated on the subculture(s) in Neo-Paganism—and I include, sadly, the very important issues of ethics, values, and politics in that term—is part of why we aren't taken seriously as a religion. Instead, we need to be asking each other hard questions about our religion itself. Even arguing about it—and yes, I am aware that arguing will be inevitable—is better than simply ignoring the whole question. If we can't explain the deeper understandings of our religion (or perhaps that should be "religions"; I'm well aware of the fragmented differences between our sects) to outsiders, it means that we do not really understand them ourselves.

This is, without question, a book on Neo-Pagan polytheistic theology, which is a subject few people seem to be interested in, including we Pagans ourselves. Neo-Paganism may have been born from a handful of mystery traditions with a succinct theological worldview, but it came of age while being flooded by religion-rejecting refugees from mainstream faiths. In fact, many of them were looking for what one such émigré enthusiastically called "...a religion for people who don't believe in religion!" Some didn't even seem to believe in gods, spirits, or anything outside of themselves, but something in Neo-Paganism—the progressive ethics, the lack of sexism and homophobia, the sex-positive and woman-positive culture, the emphasis on Nature, the associated magical traditions, the possibility of nonhierarchical groups, even the *Lord Of The Rings* aesthetic—drew them in.

One might have thought that Buddhism, with its essential atheist worldview, would be a better fit for such theological anarchists, but Buddhism came with its own difficulties—a focus on transcending rather than sacralizing the natural world, an emphasis on many hours of repetitive exercises, and centuries of Asian cultural baggage that wasn't technically part of the belief system but stubbornly stuck to it anyway. Neo-Paganism seemed like the perfect religion, except when you considered the inconvenient idea of actually believing in the reality of those ancient Pagan myths and the beings who inhabited them. Which, frankly, few of the new émigrés actually did. The myths could be easily dismissed as parables about the depth of human experience and the Gods seen as internal archetypes. One could go through the motions of a ritual because it triggered good feelings from the "collective unconscious", and never have to worry about it seeming sacrilegious. We were about praxis, not faith—a faith of doing, not believing—and many Pagans were and are fine with that concept.

Other Neo-Pagans leaned toward pantheism, panentheism, and syncretism. All the Gods are just faces of the One Divine Energy which has no identifying characteristics except for being godly, said some. It's a jewel with many facets; you only see the one that's turned to the light, but that doesn't stop it from being all part of the same over-entity. (While ideas of this sort can be drawn from many sources, the most direct route that pantheism came into modern Neo-Paganism was from the Transcendentalist and Spiritualist movements, both being heavily inspired by the Hindu philosophy of Vedanta which has long taught the essential unity of a seemingly polytheistic theology.) At the very least, there was a great deal of trouble taken to correlate deities by function, sorting them into categories that could then be squished into one many-named function-god. Even if one used many names, one was still calling on one Goddess, or one God/Goddess pairing.

This also stripped away the need for cultural context; if all love goddesses were really one love goddess seen differently by various cultures, then it didn't really matter what name you called her by or whether your offerings, rituals, or assumptions about her were harmonious to her original cultural context. Of the Pagans who could be said to believe in anything, most were pantheists. Despite the stereotypes, actual polytheists remained fairly rare until recently.

When polytheists did open their mouths, non-Pagans—and, in many cases, archetypist Pagans—were often dismissive of them as an archaic view, taking all those fairy tales too literally. For non-Pagans who were Judeo-Christian, it was ironic that ancient Western mythology was a fairy tale while Biblical stories about interactions with Yahweh and the saints were not. For those people in and out of the Pagan demographic who simply did not believe in the existence of deities as separate entities with their own agendas and means of communicating with us, polytheism simply seemed like believing in Santa or the Tooth Fairy. Adults might rapture about the archetype living in all our souls, but they didn't actually see them as discrete individual beings.

No one seemed to notice the insulting assumptions this worldview made about our ancient ancestors and their observations of the Universe. There's a German word for this concept: *Urdummheit*, the idea that everyone who lived in prehistoric or even ancient-historic times was less intelligent than modern man, and that the progression of culture has been a progression of IQ as well. By these standards, the experienced reality of thousands of years of polytheism can be quickly written off as primordial superstition by less intellectually gifted ancestors, benighted primitives who believed anything they dreamed and were prone to giving everything a fantasy explanation in order to feel less helpless in their world. Even modern politically-progressive folk who would never dream of being anything but respectful to surviving aboriginal peoples inadvertently end up engaging in *Urdummheit*, even if they would forcefully protest the idea. They weren't stupid, modern scholars are quick to point out ... just ignorant. If they'd had the ways of looking at the world that we do, they wouldn't have fallen into such foolish and childish ideas. They'd believe what we believe, say these scholars, which is in ... not much at all.

The implied insult in this kinder version of *Urdummheit* is harder to see, but still very present. The hard and inconvenient truth is that if you follow the logic, all atheism and all monotheism eventually ends up mired in *Urdummheit*. Either one believes that thousands of years of an entire world full of praying, meditating, worshiping ancestors were noticing and recounting some kind of actual reality, or they were all just idiots who weren't bright enough to figure out which of their experiences were part of an external reality and which weren't, not to mention which paid off in practical survival that helped them live long enough to become our ancestors in the first place. This is carried over in modern ethnocentric attitudes toward extant indigenous cultures and their spiritual practices; either they are just as smart as we are and their beliefs have at least some basis in reality, or the entire cultural pole around which their lives are based is simply nonsense.

In studying the history of *Urdummheit*, I waver between seeing it as standard human ego-folly, and seeing it as a tool seized upon mostly out of a need to discredit the entire religious history of the world before monotheism and later secular atheism. Perhaps it's a little of both. Regardless, religious views such as polytheism and animism are the toughest nut to crack when it comes to actually understanding and respecting the worldviews of indigenous peoples, including the ones from whom we are all descended.

But back to the Neo-Pagan dilemma. As a religion of converts—and specifically as a religion of anti-religious converts—Neo-Paganism developed a cultural ethic not only of diversity but of deliberate vagueness. After childhoods full of being told what they could and could not believe, many converts were so reactive to anything remotely seeming like a religious authority or doctrine that most Pagan groups fell back on "if it works for you, do it", with no thought of creating a standard for future group practice. No one criticized anyone's contribution, because that would be unfair, and anyway how could anyone judge someone else's spiritual experiences? In a sense, Neo-Paganism became the equivalent of the pathologically conflict-avoidant person who will smile brightly and say something soothing and meaningless in order to placate anyone who seems the least bit upset. On the other hand, some later denominations—including some reconstructionist sects and some remaining mystery traditions—reacted to this spiritual vagueness by going in the other direction and deciding that the only religious truths were the few written crumbs that escaped the Christian purge; any modern inspiration was entirely nonsensical, because the Gods weren't talking any more.

Neither of these approaches has helped the issue of developing a modern polytheistic theology. The conflict-avoidant pick-your-own-truth is great for personal spiritual practice if one intends to be an eternal solitary practitioner—and, to be fair, there's nothing wrong with that path and many people are called to it—but truths (and I deliberately use the plural for this word) have always created conflicts. Fear of proposing any absolute doctrines—or even doctrines predicated on accepting specific beliefs for the moment because they seem to work—means that one does not dare to explore serious questions about how the Gods and the Universe functions. In the other direction, there are gaps in the meager surviving written records of the ancients that leave large holes in how those serious questions were seen in their faith (and often, to echo the *Urdummheit* issue again, accompanied by an assumption that they had a simplistic view of religion and never considered asking those questions). Without comparing the divine inspiration of a great number of believers, we cannot begin to fill in those gaping holes. The assumption that the Gods no longer speak to human beings, and that they cannot understand the modern human situation, discounts the living faith experience of thousands of people.

So how do we begin to construct a theology that is authentic to our experiences, as polytheists, of how the Universe works? We can start by finding a middle ground, where we keep an open mind and are able to entertain the idea of change ... and at the same time, we are on the lookout for corroborating information, whether from ancient or modern sources.

We can also start by talking about our beliefs and experiences, and listening to each other even when we are disagreeing. This book came about because I worked up the courage to give a workshop on polytheistic theology, not from the perspective it is usually explored—a sociological and historical comparison of polytheistic world religions—but from a place of my own beliefs. It started small; people in my home Pagan church wanted religious education that was more than just comparative mythology, and more specifically, our fledgling ministry program needed a clear explanation of exactly what it was that we as a church believed, in order to work effectively as a minister from that point of view. It began with the ministry students, then other members of the church clamored for it, then one church member who was involved with a Pagan festival suggested that I take it there. Soon afterwards, I was teaching my workshop on practical, usable polytheistic theology—called by the name of this book, *Dealing*

*With Deities*—in strange cities to rooms full of people whose religious tradition I had no idea about.

After the classes, people were coming up to me and saying, "It all makes so much more sense to me now!" The most telling expressions of thanks were the people who were grateful because they'd felt that the only way to practice their polytheism was not to think too hard about it. They wanted answers that were more thoughtful than "It's all just a mystery—don't try to understand it, because you won't be able to." There was—and is—a need for coherent theological theories, even for several different ones.

For myself, I was at first profoundly uncomfortable with the idea of teaching my personal theology to others. It seemed like a huge act of hubris—what if I was wrong? What if Pagans thought that I was trying to set myself up as some kind of Pope? What if my words caused some kind of a divisive holy war? Still, the fact that I got so many positive responses—and people saying that with one class I'd changed the entire way that they saw the Gods and their religion—made me feel that perhaps this was more useful than it was hubristic or potentially troublesome. After all, Neo-Paganism has a long tradition of sampling some concepts from the religious buffet and passing on others; I had to have faith that Neo-Pagans could do the same with my pet theories.

So this is my disclaimer: Everything in this book is derived from my own experiences, and those of other polytheists with whom I compared notes. While I will be speaking from a place of "This is the way it is," please understand that this mode of speaking does not negate you, the reader, seeing things from an entirely different place. It is the way I—and many other polytheists—see the world, and that's all. So this is your disclaimer, right here: I have no expectations or assumptions that you are required to believe anything I write herein. If the worldview of myself and my spiritual compatriots rings true for you, help yourself. If it doesn't, please hear my implicit encouragement to explore for yourself and find your own way. Please hear that even when you're reading words of mine that say "This is the way it is." Understand that this means, always, "This is the way that I have experienced it, and I can speak only from this viewpoint." Refer back to this page as many times as you need in order to "refresh" your memory of this disclaimer. I'm aware that I may be, as much as any of us, one of the blind men describing the elephant's trunk ... but all of us blind men will never get a better picture if we don't compare notes about our experience of the elephant, and try to make sense of the biggest invisible elephant in our faith.

## Polytheism And Her Sisters: Defining Belief

What does it mean to be a polytheist? That answer varies between cultural groups—an indigenous person on one side of the world will experience differently than an indigenous person on the other side of the world, not to mention the added issue of those who are not living on indigenous land or practicing an unbroken ancestral tradition. However, if nothing else, disagreeing with someone can often teach you surprising things about your own perspective. However, polytheism exists as part of an array of choices, and it's important to show it as part of that array. Let's start with definitions. If you already know all these terms, skip ahead.

- **Atheism:** The belief that there is no actual single self-aware force responsible for controlling or affecting the Universe that we can comprehend in any useful way. Some people would call themselves agnostics rather than atheists, usually meaning that while they don't currently believe in anything, they are open to the possibility of something undeniable turning up in the future. It's important for Pagans to be tolerant of atheists, because part of this belief system is that our Gods need no defending. If the Gods really want a particular person to see and hear them, they'll make it happen. If it isn't happening, perhaps that person is not meant to walk the road of faith in this lifetime, or perhaps it's more important that they find it themselves than they find it at all, or some other reason. Another important thing to remember is that it is disrespectful to expect someone to believe in any God that is not speaking to them personally. They may choose to do so if they are moved to it, but they should never be forced. Our Gods don't want people forced toward or away from them, and they don't need those efforts. Atheism should be seen as a perfectly reasonable response to having had no contact with the Divine, nor being called by them to do so.

Modern Neo-Paganism may be in a corner accompanied only by Buddhism when it comes to religions with a serious percentage of followers who are openly atheist. Many Neo-Pagans come to this demographic for reasons far removed from being called by the Gods. Some are searching for a faith that supports individualism, or ecology, or sustainable living, or equal human rights, or feminism, or sexual freedom, or other values less supported in other faiths. Some are seeking to recreate the traditions of their ancestors, some are fascinated by historical recreation, and others are drawn aesthetically to the panoply and theater of the various rites and rituals. Some come to it through magical practice, via the Pagan and non-Pagan mystery traditions, and are drawn in by the trappings. Some are recruited by their spouses and partners. Some have had psychic experiences, and are looking for validation. Some are attracted to it as a "subculture", with its own fashions and values, rather than as a religion. Some are attempting to rebel against majority religions, and find Neo-Paganism sufficiently shocking to their family members. Some merely find Paganism spiritually moving as a practice, without feeling obligated to believe in the entities that are invoked in its rituals. Whatever the reason, at any given Pagan gathering, a not insignificant percentage of the people attending any ritual or workshop will not be convinced of the external reality of the Gods that others may be worshipping.

The reaction of Pagan trendsetters to this situation varies. Some are careful not to use language that will sound as if they are trying to force the reader or listener into believing in the Gods, especially since proselytizing is a social sin among most modern Pagan groups, and anything that reeks of it will be generally condemned. Others are more hard-line, using terms that assume for belief in Gods and spirits, and feel that to do otherwise would be as unthinkable as using a Christian liturgy that discounted the existence of both Jesus and Jehovah.

> ❖ **Monotheism:** The belief that there is only one deity, and all others are either minor entities that do not count as deities, or nonexistent, or delusions. This was not the original definition of monotheism, as can be seen by the fact that the Bible rails against the worship of other Gods in a way that definitely indicates that they exist. The original definition was closer to henotheism, which is a more recent term we will define next. Monotheists do not even agree on each other's Gods; some believe that all monotheists are worshipping the same God, albeit in different ways; others believe that the One God only accepts their form of worship, and all other monotheists are honoring "false Gods". Modern monotheism is, by its nature, a bit of a problem for polytheists because it claims that its God is real while all the rest of ours are not.

People will believe what they will believe for their own subjective reasons, but it's sometimes possible to carefully bring a monotheist who is not actively fearful of polytheism around to the more sensible (in our view) practice of henotheism.

- ❖ **Henotheism:** The belief that there may be many Gods, but the believer is only called to interact with one of them. As a liberal Christian friend of mine said, "I know that there are many Gods out there to choose from, and I'm sure that they are all great and rewarding in their way, but it was the Carpenter who called me, and he prefers I focus on him alone." Healthy henotheism does not feel the need to put down other Gods in order to justify focusing on their God; in fact, healthy and devoted henotheists are able to recognize the devotion of others to their Gods as a familiar emotion, and feel both secure in their own path and appreciative of the paths of others.

Henotheism can also exist within polytheism. In some polytheistic religious traditions—certain parts of Hinduism, for example—people are encouraged to dedicate themselves to one deity in pantheon, and turn to that deity for everything. They do not stop honoring other Gods, in the sense that they consider all Gods worthy of worship and they will take part in group offerings thereto (often on holidays dedicated to other deities) but they do not actively seek out any God but their own. In these cases, their conception of that deity becomes less about them being the "God of X" and more about being "my God of everything, flavored slightly with X". They expect that deity to give them advice and intervention for every part of their lives—health, money, love, fertility, war, good fortune—instead of turning to different Gods for different functions. Since this does seem to work for them, we might theorize that when someone dedicates themselves so wholly to one deity, they get hidden aspects of them that less intense worshipers may never see. (It's also possible that many of them are ending up with a "higher" and thus less specific form of that deity, which may be less personal but more diffuse. We'll talk about levels of deity in a future chapter.)

I came to henotheism from an essentially polytheistic worldview. I'd honored a variety of gods over the years, but at some point my relationship with one god, Frey, deepened and changed in a way that, as a polytheist, I had a hard time understanding. Rather than seeing Frey as one god in a set of many gods, each with their unique specialties, Frey seemed to me to simply be God. God of the World, God of all Life, God of the Body, God of the Sun, of the Rain, of the Trees, God of Everything. I know that many of the roles I attribute to Frey properly "belong" to other gods, but for me that is only an intellectual understanding. I don't feel Thor's presence in the rain, or Sunna's in the sun, or Laufey's in the trees. I feel Frey in everything.

Or at least, nearly everything. While Frey is God to me, he isn't the "One God" in a universal monotheistic or pantheistic sense. He still has a certain personality, certain attributes, and certain preferences, and if there are certain things that he *is* then there are certain things that he *is not*.

This means that there are some things and forces in the world that I attribute to other gods, but with very few exceptions, those things have little spiritual depth or relevance to me. The other gods I see as a polytheist would, but I don't tend to look for them. They are not God to me.

– Joshua Tenpenny, US Pagan

One might call upon another deity once in a great while for some practical need that falls under that God's influence (such as a henotheistic devotee of Shiva who happens to be a shopkeeper asking Lakshmi to bring customers to his shop, or a henotheistic devotee of Artemis who wants to ask for a friend to find the right husband). However, all the general needs that make people turn to spirituality are met entirely by one's patron deity.

Metaphorically, we could look at it like this: You might have three or four advice needs in a day, and you might call three or four different professionals for advice, or you might call your parents and ask them because they're your parents, and you just call on them for advice about all sorts of things. You know that you can bend their ear and they'll be generous about it, because of your personal relationship with them. (If you don't have a good relationship with your parents, substitute "best friend" or even "spouse".) If they can't answer, they may even go out of their way to ask around for you, something they wouldn't do if they were the professional and you were the client calling on the phone. On the other hand, sometimes you will have to call a professional if Mom and Dad don't know anything about fly-fishing.

For polytheistic henotheists like me, it's more like this kind of arrangement. We honor other deities in group worship, and occasionally interact with them as "specialists", but our patron deity is our patron deity for a reason. The relationship exists because we suit each other so well, so they are our primary points of contact.

– A.J., US Pagan

- ❖ **Pantheism:** The belief that although there may be more than one manifestation of deity, they are all part of one larger Godhead. Some versions of pantheism posit that all living things are also part of this Godhead, that we are as integral to it as any deity, and that any personalized, human-type deity is merely a specific mask on the larger force of Divine Power. One individual put it like this: "The divine force is like a gemstone with many facets, and we just happen to see the facet that is turned to the light at any given time, but the facets are not separable; they are just an illusion. The whole is what's real and what's important." Some pantheists, however, will acknowledge that while they may believe that all Gods are part of One Higher Being, some people get much more personal satisfaction—and results—out of "acting as if" there were highly separated Gods and calling on them.

While pantheism can exist in the same worldview with polytheism to an extent (read the chapter on "Going Higher"), it falls down when it comes to understanding the need to treat Gods and spirits as individuals with their own (nonhuman) agendas. It's fine for a distant (or transcendent) relationship with Gods, but can become problematic in a practical way (from a polytheistic viewpoint) in the rare event that the individual is approached by very distinct Gods. I say "rare" because in my experience the Gods are not offended at all by pantheism. They simply seem to give like for like, and if someone sees them as not having a separate nature, they don't ever come up close and personal enough to dissuade them of the notion. In contrast, there is an underlying assumption in "hard" polytheist belief that to conflate Gods and spirits will insult them, and that they will not fully manifest if one is not fully believing in them as separate entities and addressing them appropriately. The metaphor that is often used by hard polytheists to explain their stance is: "If I owe you ten bucks, and I say that humanity is all one anyway and I give the ten bucks to Bob over there, you're not going to be pleased."

As we'll see in the chapters on levels of deity, it is possible to understand Gods as having both very separate and human aspects, as well as more blurred and less human ones—polytheism blending into pantheism somewhere at the top. This is often referred to as "soft polytheism", as opposed to "hard polytheism" which concentrates on the Gods as entirely separate individuals. Some hard polytheists don't even indulge in occasional semi-pantheism by conflating minor aspects of deities (such as Aphrodite Genetrix and Aphrodite Porne, or the Norse Odin and the Germanic Woden); in this belief, every single deity is separate from every other, and deserves to be treated in this manner. One could be a soft polytheist in one's theoretical view of the Universe, and a hard polytheist in practice because it works for whatever you're doing. One could also be a hard polytheist in group practice and a soft polytheist in private practice, or the reverse. Some Pagan henotheists that I know are hard polytheists in group worship where they may hail other Gods, but feel that their patron deity wants them to see Him/Her on a more pantheistic level, as their connection to the All. In general, the message that they have received was not that polytheism was an inaccurate reflection of the Universe, but that it was not the focus that they were to have for this period of time.

- ❖ **Panentheism:** A subset of pantheism, panentheism believes that while all things are part of God, God is present as an outside force as well, and is more than merely the sum of the divinity of all things. "God is the ocean and we are a fish swimming in that, as opposed to God is the sum total of the divinity of all fish," one priest put it. This is another alternative to monotheism that some people in traditional monotheistic religions may turn to. In this view, the separate deities of polytheism could be seen as facets of their external God, or as nonexistent, depending on their religious background.

- ❖ **Animism:** The belief that not only all living things, but all natural things, and some man-made things, have an indwelling spirit/soul of their own. Animism can be polytheistic (the spirits are all separate and have their own specific identities) or pantheistic (the spirits are all part of the universal energy, and merely have their own flavor).

While not all polytheists are animists as well, a great many of them are, especially ones who follow older indigenous faiths and/or work with a wide array of non-divine spirits as well as Gods.

- ❖ **Archetypism:** A form of atheism that believes that divine archetypes are either psychologically rich internal structures that are spiritually useful for self-improvement, or specific flavors of universal energy that can be worked with in order to gain personal power. Archetypists may discuss the Gods or spirits as a "being-ness", a mythical way of being rather than a specific entity (such as the average Jungian psychologist talks about). Many of the archetypists who see the Gods as "energy constructs" believe that they were created artificially by human belief, and will cease to exist when there are no more humans believing in them. Some archetypists, while not exactly believing in the Gods and spirits as actual entities, will acknowledge that many people find suspending one's belief and "acting as if" one believes in them to be spiritually useful, because the "child self" or unconscious still believes in miracles and wonders and "make-believe" people and will respond emotionally to a ritual that invokes them. Archetypism also tends to be found where Neo-Paganism borders with demographics interested in psychology, self-help, and New Age spirituality, although the last group also tends to be high in pantheism. One polytheist writer referred to experiencing the sacred archetype of a deity as "standing in their shadow", which makes a good deal of sense from a polytheistic perspective. Standing in their shadow, however, is not the same as touching them ... but it may be as close as some people are comfortable with getting, and that's not necessarily a bad thing for them.

Archetypism is fairly problematic when it runs headlong into polytheism, more so than plain old atheism, and again the culprit is the polytheist perception of offending the Gods. To disbelieve in a God because you've never personally met them is one thing, and fairly understandable. To believe that you've actually met the deity that someone else is worshipping, and that you think it is really a human-created energy-form to be used as a tool, is quite another. From a hard polytheistic perspective, this can appear almost like a sociopathic treatment of the Gods, reducing real and much beloved People to mere objects to be exploited.

I would, again, caution polytheists from getting overemotional about the issue, and remind them that our very real Gods need no defending. First of all, they are Gods, with all that implies—they are not exploitable in that way. Second, while we do not see our Gods as omniscient, they are certainly older and wiser and more experienced that we are. They understand that someone who does not believe in their existence is certainly inadvertent in any offense they may give. Third, in my experience, our very real Gods rarely bother with archetypists at all, so no one is actually being harmed. Remember, again, that if the Gods wished to change those people's minds, they would find a way to do it.

At one point in the past, a group of archetypists rented my back field to do their ritual. They were polite and didn't leave trash around, so I was fine with letting them have it. Out of courtesy, they invited me to attend, and gave me a copy of the ritual to peruse. As I read their very archetypist view of the Gods, complete with ordering them down to give various favors and conflating large groups of deities from different cultures who barely resembled each other, I wondered if I should attend. The voice from my patron deity came immediately: *No.* Surprised, I asked if this was offensive to Her and to other Gods. *No,* she said. *They don't know any better, so we don't care. But you know better. From your mouth, those words would be an offense.*

Some Pagan theologians and sociologists divide the "traditions" (what other faiths might call "sects" or "denominations") of Neo-Paganism into five basic varieties: Traditional British Wicca, Modern Wicca, Wiccan-derived traditions, reconstructionists, and reconstructionist-derived traditions. Of the lot, reconstructionists (groups who are attempting to reconstruct the ancient religions of specific cultures, e.g. Norse/Germanic traditions such as Asatru or Heathenry, Roman groups such as Religio Romana, Hellenic groups such as Hellenion, Egyptian traditions such as Kemet) tend to be the most polytheistic in order to recreate the strong polytheism of the ancients. Reconstructionist-derived groups range from extremely polytheistic to somewhere vaguely between polytheism and pantheism, but generally work with more than one culture or pantheon of deities.

In their article *Pagan Deism: Three Views,*[1] Margarian Bridger and Stephen Hergest posit (albeit only in a Wiccan paradigm) polytheism, pantheism, and archetypism as points on a triangle, with a spectrum of belief between each point. In this view, some Pagans fall on the continuum between polytheism and pantheism (the Gods are sometimes separate and sometimes not, to varying extents), or between pantheism and archetypism (the Gods may be creations of our minds, but there is also sometimes a divine force behind those thought-forms). The line between polytheism and archetypism is a bigger and more mind-boggling stretch, as these seem like the "most theistic" and "most atheistic" points. Bridger and Hergest suggest only that this continuum might belong to people who have deep and personal relationships with thought-form deities that they don't actually believe in; others have commented that it might belong to people who believe in the Gods, but believe that the "being" they experience in their spiritual interactions is a human construct which has some connection to the related deity, but is not a direct manifestation of that deity.

To date, the Neo-Pagan demographic has only occasionally come to strife and argument over the differing points of belief listed above. Part of this is due to the social ethic of religious tolerance prevalent in Neo-Paganism today (which, admittedly, varies from group to group), but part of it is due to the fact that serious Pagan theological study and comparative writing is still in its infancy within our own faiths, and not yet taken seriously enough by outside faiths to be worthy of comparative study by reputable interfaith theologians. This situation will inevitably change as more deep writing and discussion is created and discussed across religious lines (a maturation of faith which is already occurring), and as Neo-Paganism continues to grow in numbers. And, frankly, I'm looking forward to that. Polytheism is the most difficult of all these "sisters" to describe in depth theology, but that doesn't mean that it can't be done, thoroughly and beautifully and with all due love and reverence.

---

[1] *Pagan Deism: Three Views*, Bridger and Hergest, *The Pomegranate: The International Journal of Pagan Studies*, Volume #1, February, 1997, pp. 37-42.

## The Nature Of Deities

Throughout this book you will hear me use the term "Gods and spirits". I anticipate a certain amount of confusion with that at first, if only because it begs the question of what is a God and what is a spirit, and where is the line drawn? The answer is one of those answers that I don't have, exactly, although I will touch on the issue throughout this book. It seems to be not so much a line as a grey area, and a very subjective one at that. In Vodou, for example, the *lwa* are referred to as spirits rather than Gods, even though their powers are such that many Neo-Pagans would consider them the latter ... but Vodou has a "God", an impersonal being above all the *lwa* who generally doesn't talk to people (and who occasional scholars believe is a result of Vodou's merging with Catholicism), and if that being is God, no other being can take that title according to that religious tradition. In contrast, some ancient peoples worshiped as Gods beings with a more limited scope than the *lwa*—local land-Gods or river-Gods, for example.

When people talk about interactions with a God, generally the awe in their voice has to do with scope. It is a presence that feels so much bigger than us, whereas there are plenty of spirits who are the same size or smaller, so to speak. This, however, is still a very subjective decision, and it can be affected by the perceptiveness (or distance) of the human being involved. It can also be affected by how much of a connection a deity has to this world; some are more interested in (or have more vested interest in, or have a more powerful connection to) our heavy material human world than others. It can also be affected by how much of a connection a deity has to the individual person in their Presence.

### Beginnings

How are Gods born? Some of them are born of other Gods, just as we are born of personal parents. Others seem to come into being out of the stuff of the Universe, perhaps a coalescence of Being-ness that eventually develops a more complex self-awareness. Some may have started out as elementals or other not-quite-Gods and gained a "higher" aspect over time; this can even happen to dead human beings, on rare occasions. This is not to say that the euhemerization of Gods is always accurate; trying to claim that they are all simply the lost legends of mere human beings whose stories were passed down and changed beyond recognition ignores (perhaps deliberately) ancestral accounts of the existence of Otherworlds and the many millennia that humans have been walking in and out of them. However, in some cases an ancestor can—with the help of the Gods and, one would assume, a great deal of spiritual development on their part—become one of their junior members. It is attested to in so many mythologies that it would be unwise to discount the idea.

One example of this would be the worship of Antinous, who is—as his modern devotees call him—the youngest member of the Roman pantheon of Gods. Antinous was a young man, said to be "wise beyond his years", who was loved by an Emperor. When he died in his early twenties, the grief-stricken Emperor Hadrian had him deified—an entirely unprecedented move for someone who had been of non-Imperial origin—and encouraged a cult around worshiping him. The cult of Antinous flourished for some years until Christianity took it down with all the other Roman religions, but modern devotees have taken it up again ... and report that Antinous is just as divine and present for them as he was to his ancient devotees.

There is also the question of human beings creating an idea—perhaps in literature or media—and that if enough people worship that idea, it will become an entity and then a deity. While I am not utterly opposed to the idea that this could happen, it would probably take a lot of people a very long time. It is also possible that some other deity, perhaps one whose name we have forgotten, might step forth and take on that created role as an aspect of itself. Many polytheists have theorized that when a pantheist calls on a nonspecific deity such as The Love Goddess, rather than getting a general undifferentiated higher entity, they get instead a differentiated love goddess who chooses to come forward, answer the "phone", and step into the "Great Love Goddess" role. It's not so much of a far stretch to imagine that a deity might step up and don the image of a popular archetype once people begin actually worshiping it.

However, it is also clear from many accounts that the direction of such evolution is not only in the direction of transcendence. It is important to remember that in this world view, everything goes in circles. There is no one-way linear perfection. We may not see much of the other side of that cycle, but we can be assured that it exists. Lesser spirits may evolve toward Gods, and Gods may evolve toward higher impersonal transcendence (perhaps over a period of time that our minds are completely unable to grasp with any meaning) but at some point there has to be a re-collapse and a rotting down, in order for there to be new growth. It may be that parts of the impersonal All are continually separating off and becoming the most barely self-aware of Being-ness, eventually to grow up to be something much more complex and self-aware, and then slowly evolve up to lose their self-ness and merge back into the All, and restart the cycle. It is also possible that Gods can fall back down, over time and with the vagaries of whatever passes for "age" for a God, to simple elemental forms, and further still. We don't know exactly how that works for them, but perhaps it is because we have been too fixated on the idea of Gods as eternal and unchanging, and haven't actually been looking.

## Divine Essentials

One way to comprehend the nature of the Gods—and how their nature is different from ours—is to understand that they are more fully themselves than we are. By this I mean that even the most complex deities (and some of them can be awfully complex) are more wholly monolithic as entities than we humans are. We tend to be much more muddled up with outside influences, and our various aspects are rarely wholly clear in and of themselves. Gods are much more precisely and purely what they are, without extraneous matter in their personalities. Yes, some deities have what seem to be contradictions in their natures ... but in every case I've personally investigated, when I spoke with a human being who was devoted to such a deity, they have spoken to me about part of that deity's Mystery being about revealing the underlying truth that unites those supposed contradictions.

What makes a God, in essence, is that they are a pure embodiment of some part of universal essence (or could easily be in a heartbeat, if they were deciding to act from their highest self) and, beyond that, they hold full knowledge of that piece of essence and the implications of all its results. Those two qualities could be considered the "markers" of divinity, and we'll discuss them separately.

Gods are, as we will discuss in the chapter on vertical aspects of deity, capable of instantly moving up and down the scale from personal to transpersonal consciousness in a way that is heartbreakingly difficult for us mortals, and even their most human aspects have the "feel" of that universal essence, like a light shining through a translucent filter that could be pulled aside at a moment's notice. One could say—as many religious theorists have—that all human beings are also pure embodiments of some part of universal essence, which would make us all just mini-gods.

While that theory may make us feel better, there is still the very real difference of scale. If we and the Gods are all just lights shining through, we have been placed here to manifest that light through a very, very dense material. Saint-types and avatar-types may have a thinner material, but Gods have only the sheerest of veils, and they can whisk them aside if need be. While it's a point of hope to theorize about the divine within all of us, it does not eradicate the gap between us and Them. Nor does claiming that we are just like the Gods actually help us to get any closer to our higher selves.

> I have come to grasp that human beings carry a spark of Source, but it's packaged and layered with tons of matter. I mentally visualize that Source stuff as white, because it has all the colors. We humans are tiny carriers of that, but we are only carriers. To me, Deity is a very pure and strong manifestation of one of the colors, or a mix of the colors—sort of like specialist version of the white stuff. So if we were to see a Deity as, let's say, green—or in my patron goddess's case, deep purple or aubergine; She manifests aubergine fully, one hundred per cent, but it's only aubergine. My white stuff has got aubergine in there, in a minuscule amount, clothed in many layers of non-divine stuff. If I were to fully ascend to a higher level and be one with the Source, I would outrank her, but if I went there, at that point there would be no more Me. I would no longer exist as myself.
>
> In order to exist individually as myself, I have agreed to serve, learn from, and submit to Gods, who are the pure, specialist forms of the colors. So when I serve Deity, I do it as a human being. My patron deity's job, then, is to force me—because I tend to have to be forced—up the evolutionary ladder. She is the closest thing I have to a pure manifestation of the Source that I can reach and interact with, because the Source itself won't talk to you directly as a human being.
>
> So I serve Her because both of us are manifested from the same Source, and that Source in the end has the final say. It's the natural order of things that until your soul has reached that state of purity, you need a manifestation that you can grab onto in order to get

you there. Her job is to purify me in order to help me grow and ascend, and to be my point of reference, my connection for interaction with the divine. My job as a priestess, among others, is to be a point of connection for people who cannot yet directly interface with a God or Goddess, just as She is my connection because I cannot directly interface with the Source.

– Lydia Helasdottir, Pagan in Germany

## The Flaws In The Gem

The stone that we call a beryl, in its purest form, is entirely colorless. It is its flaws that give it color and turn it into an emerald or an aquamarine. This is an analog to what it means when we say that even the flaws of the Gods are holy. By being so entirely and wholly and perfectly their own piece of Universal Being, they will of course have the flaws that are the other side of that coin. A deity that is a master craftsperson may well be focused to the point of forgetting the needs of loved ones. A deity that is entirely dedicated to feelings (such as a goddess of love or marriage) will not always react with rational objectivity to their own pain. A deity that must make hard decisions based on the long-term good (such as a god of death or justice) must sometimes be cold and unmerciful in the short term. The mistakes that the Gods make—and mythology certainly shows them as making many harmful mistakes—can partly be explained by the understanding that these were the decisions of the more human aspect of the Gods (an issue that we'll get into in the following chapter), but only partly, and to leave it there is to miss the point.

To say that a God manifests the divine nature of a character flaw is to reaffirm that all things in Nature are sacred, and that includes destruction. All things have a destructive as well as a creative or sustaining side—the ocean gave us life but can drown us, the earth can feed us or open up and swallow us, etc.—and that destructive side is part of the nature of that Being-ness, and cannot be separated off, any more than a Sun that you could gaze upon without damage to your eyes would be able to give enough light to make this world the green bounty that it is. It's not about being "part good and part bad"—again, that's a concept from a different sort of religion. In polytheistic Paganism, we see such labeling as a view that is biased toward human convenience rather than the larger scope of nature. We want to get beyond that, which means getting beyond our own pain about the imperfections in the world that hurt us—including the apparent imperfections of the Gods.

A deity can be divine in her jealousy (like Hera), or in his fury (like Odin), or in her depression (like Demeter), or in his sheer overwhelming desire to destroy (like Fenris). We don't want to be in the path of these divine emotions, any more than we want to be in the way of a tsunami, but sometimes tsunamis happen and that's life. The protocols we set up to deal respectfully and in right relationship with Gods are akin to the early-warning radar system in this case, or perhaps a better metaphor might be a natural disaster that we have some hope of ameliorating or turning aside—some of the time, at least.

It is true, however, that we are the children of the Gods. (In some cases this is literal, but in all cases it is figurative—we are their Younger Kin, and their fondness for us stems from this fact.) We have those same divine destructive urges in ourselves, whether we like to admit it or not. Perhaps we don't have them on such a grand scale, but even our small scale is big enough to devastate our lives and the well-being of those around us. The Gods, like us, are subject to the laws of consequence, and thus we can learn from their mistakes, writ large for us to see.

If some Gods seem to escape consequences for their actions, that may only be because our knowledge of their stories is incomplete. There are plenty of consequence-stories still on the books, though—Apollo indulges his unready, wayward son out of love and lets him drive the sun-chariot, and loses him in the process. Inanna lets her immature, wayward consort rule her kingdom while she journeys to the Underworld, and ends up having to sacrifice him when she returns. Coyote continually looks for the shortcut and it ends in catastrophe about half the time. The *orisha* of the African-diaspora Lukumí religion, for example, all seem to have redemption bound up in their myths: Obatala is the reformed alcoholic, Shango is the redeemed murderer, Ogun the redeemed rapist, Oya the redeemed jealous wife. Each makes terrible mistakes, comes to grief for them, and finds a way to atone or move beyond them.

Dealing with these difficult qualities in ourselves—each of which is simply the other side of a coin whose opposite face we value—often results in us dissociating from them, deciding that they are *other* and not really part of who we are. We lock them in our mental psychological basements and deny that they exist, or that they have any value. In doing so, we lose our ability to love and value ourselves wholly, and begin the seed of self-loathing in our souls. Once we've begun that route—which everyone who understands themselves walks down at some point—we paradoxically lose our ability to wholly redeem ourselves. If we cannot love ourselves as we are rather than what we would prefer to be—love ourselves with no hope, either, of changing ourselves—then we lose hope of fully changing. One cannot redeem one's self from a place of self-loathing; one has to come to deep self-forgiveness first. It's one of those mysterious contradictions of Life, a mystery which the flaws of the Gods can help us through. To see them wholly, including the parts of their natures which make us uncomfortable, and to love and worship them anyway—and, most important, to forgive them for being imperfect and thus see their imperfections as no impediment to worship—holds up the lantern to the path of loving and forgiving their echoes in ourselves.

> I think that there is a very important core theological difference between polytheism and monotheism (or at least Christianity) that often gets overlooked. Polytheists tend to see the Gods as reflections of *nature as it is*, rather than ideals of *human nature at its best*. There is no direct analogue to the "What Would Jesus Do?" concept. Polytheists don't generally believe that to be a better person, you should in all ways strive to act like Deity X. We might admire certain traits in Deity X, and strive to emulate them in those ways, but we also recognize that trying to be like them all the time in all ways isn't going to work out well for us as human beings.
>
> – A.J., US Pagan

## Power, Knowledge, and Wisdom

It's also important to refrain from mistaking mere power for divine nature. Just because some entities have amassed a certain amount of power does not mean that they are more divine—i.e. closer to being a clear aspect of the universal essence, with all its attendant wisdom. This is similar to how the gaining of temporal power by a human being does not necessarily imply more wisdom on their part—although they may well be wise in the ways of gaining and wielding temporal power, and could be usefully consulted on that matter. It's a matter of scope of wisdom. At some point, characteristics move from "this being has divine power" to "this being *is* a divine power". That divine scope of wisdom is the second characteristic of a deity, and it is what we will look at now.

When I say that a God/dess holds "full knowledge of that piece of essence and the implications of all its results", I mean that they have fully comprehensive knowledge *of their field*. That may include far-reaching specific knowledge such as, for example, where your personal destiny intersects with that field, or the potential physical and spiritual consequences of any activity or decision even remotely connected with that field. It's not omniscience, but it is certainly a further gaze than we can muster. A love goddess, for instance, may not know everything about warfare (with the exception of love goddesses who also had that as one of their aspects, of which there are a few), but she will know all the love-relationship possibilities in your life, and what paths lead to and away from them. She will also know whether any of those love relationships are meant to be crucial lessons in your life that you Must Not Miss, or whether the important destined moments for you are not in her sphere of influence. If there are any in the first category, she will know if you signing up for a stint in the military overseas will interfere with you intersecting those possible loves, and she will advise (or push, or manipulate) accordingly. She will understand, with a fullness that you may find it difficult to comprehend, all your blocks to intimacy and relationship, and what steps you will have to make in order to get past them, and what people would be best to lead you down that path. (This is on top of her knowledge of everything to do with all forms of Love and how they manifest in the world.) With her scope of understanding, she doesn't need to know anything about military service to come to you in a dream and say, "This is not where you're supposed to be going right now."

An entity can be powerful within its own limited sphere, and yet not a God because it does not have that comprehensive knowledge. An elemental spirit of Fire, for example, has a comprehensive knowledge of Fire and all the ways that it manifests, but does not have the knowledge of all further implications such as where and when Fire will intersect with your particular thread of destiny, or what the far-reaching consequences of Fire will be on that city over there. If it did, it would be a Fire God.

In addition, Gods can *learn* on a greater scale than that of, say, elemental spirits or dead human souls. They can pick up outside knowledge that they might not otherwise have had, even information outside their scope of practice. We, and our senses, are sources of that knowledge. When the Gods get the chance to experience life through our eyes and minds, they learn. As they are not omniscient, they cannot see the mind and experience of every human being, all the time. However, when they "connect" with us, we are doors to them just as they are doors to us. Our doors open onto our sensory experiences, our thoughts, our language, and our destinies. They can check our "file in the Akashic Records", as it were. Because they are Gods, it is easy for them to assimilate and fully comprehend that information through that connection—certainly much easier than it is for us to assimilate and comprehend what comes through to us from their end—but they cannot come to it without making some kind of connection with us.

We may not notice the moment of connection, of course. It might come to us in a dream that we may or may not remember. It might be that moment of pure joy we experience when we admire some aspect of Nature or Life. It might be when we pass through some place dear to them, or interact with someone who is being used as their eyes and ears at the moment. It might be when we pray, even if we don't feel anything in return due to our own internal clutter. It might be during a ritual when they are invoked, even if we are just watching politely and distantly from the sidelines. When we aren't distracted and we do notice that moment of connection and Presence, it is often felt through the body. Our bodies react in a certain way when we are in the presence of the Holy Powers, a way that the mental sock puppets in our heads cannot duplicate. At that moment, they Know us ... and do not think that they do not learn from us, because they do.

In our observations—and the observations of millennia of human beings—the Gods work in subtle as well as direct ways. Lois McMaster Bujold commented, in one of her fiction books, that the Gods are parsimonious, and this is definitely true. A single action by a deity will often have several effects: their long-term goals for this world, their long-term goals for their interaction with you, your short-term goals, your highest good, their highest good, and all these considerations for anyone else whom the action may impact. Often we can't even see the full effects of something that they do with us or ask us to do until a long time has passed, if ever. They are masters of managing the ripple effect in ways that we cannot even manage to see from our small mortal viewpoint, which argues strongly in favor of their ability to see higher and further than us. The source of their wisdom is not omniscience, but vantage point; the source of their miraculous effects is not omnipotence, but skill in handling the play of action and consequence, for which the former skill is necessary.

It is said that they have no hands in this world but ours, but I would expand that to saying that they have no hands in this world but ours and those of any other spirit that they can get to cooperate, even for a moment. We need to remember, over and over again, that the polytheistic world view is one of relationship, not isolation. We are all in relationship with the multitudinous components of a vast web of being, even when we are too self-absorbed to see it. Similarly, no deity is alone in the Universe, and unlike us, they are much more aware of all the other beings with whom they share the Web, and much better able to make use of those relationships. A deity may nudge human hands—witting or unwitting—to do a job, or they may engage the services of elemental beings, or subtle entities that we haven't even begun to categorize or explore. The synchronous effects that they are able to pull off in order to get our oblivious attention—and anyone who has been the subject of the gaze of a deity trying to get their attention will attest to the impressive level of subtle spectacle they can pull off—come from the pulling of all those unseen strings.

This brings us back again to the venue of not-quite-Gods, which have their own chapter later in this book, but who must make an appearance again with reference to this point. Wherever each person decides to draw the Deity/spirit line, it is important not to dismiss the contribution of spirits that fall beneath that line. Just as it is true that adults are not necessarily the only ones with wisdom, it is true that a closer-to-Earth spirit may have a much more specific message for us. As my friend Del once wrote, "One can gain wisdom from watching insects or planets." Ancestral souls may have specific knowledge of one's bloodline and spiritual inheritance, both positive and negative. Elemental spirits may have clear knowledge of the ecosystem you are in at the moment, and both your impact on it and its impact on you. While their wisdom may not be as huge in scope, such "smaller" spirits may still have things to teach you.

> For me, the distinction between "god" and "not-god" has nothing to do with power and everything to do with breadth of vision. I'll use the analogy of a forest. A given land spirit will be intimately connected to, say, a certain tree. That spirit will know everything there is to know about that tree: know how to help it grow, know how to sustain it, and know how to end it once its time has passed. If I want information about that tree I'll ask the spirit—who better? But if you ask the spirit what's happening on the other side of the

hill it couldn't tell you, because the tree is all it knows. I can see many trees as I walk along my path, and rivers and flowers and animals too, but I see only the surface—I don't know any of them intimately, and I only know what I've seen and experienced along the way.

Ancestors know not only the path I've walked, they know every path in the whole forest. Their information isn't necessarily any deeper than mine, but it is much more extensive. They also get the whole thing of being human—they know when I need to rest, how important it is to find water, and why I'm scared out here in the forest at night. If I want to make camp I'll ask them for assistance, because they know what will work best. However, they don't know the paths that haven't been walked yet, and they don't know anything beyond the forest.

Gods see the forest in its entirety, and They see how that forest relates to the mountains and deserts and seas. It's like They can see the whole map, and this allows Them to give me amazing guidance. But a god doesn't understand what it's like to walk along the path with your own two feet, and how tired and hungry you can get as you go—and They certainly don't get the specifics of each individual tree.

All of these entities have their own wisdom to share, and ultimately I think all of them directly influence my growth. The Ancestors know where I've been and offer history, the land spirits know where I'm standing at the eternal "now", and Gods know where I'm going and can see future potentials. To my way of thinking, emphasizing one over another is counterproductive, as all three perspectives are equally important to my long-term spiritual development. It really is a case where bigger is not necessarily better. If *any* of them ask me to do something or make a suggestion in their area of expertise I'll pay strict attention, because they are all wiser in their particular areas than I.

– Caer, US Pagan

## Worshiping Our Gods

The word "worship" comes from the early Anglo-Saxon *worthscipe*—to give worth to something; to imbue it with worth. What, though, does that mean in practice, when we speak of worshiping our Gods? I'll try to get it down to a simple, short paragraph:

> *To worship our Gods is to consciously recognize their inherent holiness, and to take action that celebrates that. It is to demonstrate our reverence, respect, or devotion—any or all of these. It is to give them our love, however we define that.*

There is a difference, however, in the way that we think about of our Gods that confuses many monotheists. We don't conceive of our many Gods as being either omnipotent or omniscient. They are powerful, certainly, but they are also limited. They can be remarkably human in some ways, and no one of them could be called upon for every purpose or for every person. To be a polytheist is to be comfortable with that fact, and to see our Gods no less deserving of worship simply because none of them are the Architect of the Universe. This is bewildering to people in other faiths who have been taught that their God's omniscience and omnipotence was the justification for offering worship. Many of us polytheists have been on the receiving end of a theological argument whose main issue is someone asking, "Why would you worship anything that *wasn't* omnipotent?" Since this is such a matter of perplexity for monotheists, it behooves me to try to give some useful answers about that.

❖ We recognize that holiness is not contingent upon perfection. (If that were the case, none of us flawed human beings could ever achieve even a small amount of holiness.) Something—or Someone—can be imperfect and yet still very much an example of sacredness, in their own way. We also recognize that worthiness of reverence, respect, or love is also not contingent upon perfection. After all, we love each other, and we are all limited and flawed.

❖ The Gods can be examples to learn from, and there is little that a flawed human can learn from a perfect, all-knowing being about how to manage their flaws and find holiness in spite of them. Also, flaws can make a God more beautiful, as we've mentioned that a flaw in a precious gem can make it more beautiful. Loving an imperfect God can be the first step in loving our own imperfect selves.

❖ If we see the Gods as being more powerful and knowledgeable than us (perhaps by a factor of a thousandfold) but still limited in their ability to do and know everything, we do not have to wrestle with the monotheistic bugaboo of why bad things happen if God could stop them all. Monotheistic religion spends a huge amount of effort in theological gyrations on this subject. Does God enjoy suffering? Does God simply not care? Wouldn't the first option make God evil and sadistic, and the second make God remote and unreachable? Polytheists see things differently, in ways that make these questions irrelevant. We know that the Gods do their best, but they still have to contend with a Universe with greater circumstances that sometimes thwart even them—not to mention the issue of human free will. (Of course, thoughtful polytheists and monotheists alike will probably tend to assume that there may be unexplained reasons for painful events rather than figuring that the Divine Force could have stopped it and simply let them down.)

❖ As most polytheistic religions are very earth-centered and nature-centered, we see the Divine reflected in Nature—and in Nature, there are thousands of smaller forces working in concert (and sometimes against each other). We can theorize a great Divine Watchmaker-mind behind all those smaller forces, but the likelihood of that Force being close enough to—or interested enough in—our existence seems unlikely to us. It also seems obvious to us that it is in working with those smaller forces that we can gain understanding and cause change on a level relevant to our lives. (This also brings in the idea that different Gods may work against each other, just like different parts of the natural world, and each force may win or lose the struggle in a given situation.)

- Bringing together the last two points, since our assumption is that the Gods don't have an infinite amount of power (their resources may be vast, but not unlimited), we're more likely to have a concept that certain divine interventions require more effort than others. There is a common (though not universal) understanding among polytheists that the Gods *are* natural, and the means by which they act are also natural, if subtle and mindbogglingly hard to fully comprehend, so not all interventions are equally effortless. We're also more likely to believe that there are forces like Fate and Universal Laws which restrict the actions of the Gods, or at least require a huge amount of effort to work against. Cultural theologies differ on this, but it isn't uncommon for polytheists to believe that the Fates outrank the Gods.

How do we worship our Gods? There are many different possibilities, but some of them include:

- Learning about them. If you read the excellent book *Six Ways Of Being Religious* by Dale Cannon, you'll see that this is the scholar's path. Learning everything you can about your favorite God/dess can be an act of worship for them.

- Meditating on them, while being open to possible connection and communication with them. This can also include other acts designed to form a discipline of personal devotion. (This is the Path of Devotion in Cannon's book.)

- Sharing food and drink, as libations.

- Making gifts for them—sacred handcrafts, songs, poetry, stories, regalia for their altars and their special priests.

- Performing music or dancing or ritual for them. (This is the Path of Ritual in Cannon's book.)

- Joining religious groups that are dedicated to them, whether as one of many Gods or as a special mystery tradition just for one or a few deities.

- ❖ Building a space in the world for them to send their energy through, whether that be a simple altar or a large public temple.

- ❖ For those who feel called to it, dedicating one's life to them as their representative in the world.

- ❖ Creating action in the world that they would approve of—for example, supporting organic farming in honor of an agricultural God, or veterans' aid in honor of a war God.

- ❖ Trying one's best to walk the path that one's Gods have pointed out, and listening to their advice on how best to accomplish this path, even when it is difficult. This is perhaps the most intimate form of worship—trusting them with the direction of your life.

At this point, I must stop and answer the question that is probably in the minds of any monotheists reading this book: How do polytheists see the Jewish or Christian YHWH, or the Muslim Allah? The answer depends on how antagonistic their history is with monotheistic religion, of course; people with emotional baggage about their bad childhood religious experiences, or who have been the target of religious bigotry or narrow-mindedness, are going to have a more heated and less objective view. However, I'm only going to speak from my own viewpoint, which is fairly neutral on the subject. I see him as one God among many (and, indeed, the infamous insistence on being addressed as male for most of his written history, while problematic for many modern Jews and Christians, is for me a pretty clear indicator that he has a gender, and thus is simply a single limited male god) who managed to collect a great many worshipers, and who—alone among other Gods of his era—refuses to get along with or acknowledge any other divinities. From reading the Old Testament, it is clear that he has a personality, and as many distinct flaws as any of our Gods. He is not the distant and remote Architect of the Universe. He is no more, and no less, deserving of freely given worship than any of our Gods; my only issue is the history of forced worship and conformation to his rules that his followers claim they have been doing on his orders.

We polytheists don't generally choose to play games of "my God is bigger and better than your God", with the exception of a few of us who are still carrying around patterns from certain monotheistic religions. First of all, there's no way to prove it. If you say this to me, well, first I have to accept that you're not mistaken, and that's a huge leap. Second, there's the question of whether your God is mistaken or lying. Since we believe that both are theoretically possible, there's little to go on except for the thousands of years of precedent when it comes to studying the way that Gods work, and up until the monotheistic God began forbidding such questioning, the obvious answer was that this new God was one among many, even though he refused to admit that.

Another of our understood truths is that all things are in relationship with each other, and that includes Gods and spirits. The spirit of that waterfall may be deeply bonded with the spirit of the forest that surrounds it. The spirit of the land under my house may look up to the spirit of the local mountain. That deity there may have a spouse, or lovers, or friends, or children, or parents. What happens when one of our Gods is mistaken or lies? The same thing that ideally happens when we do it—our loved ones take us to task for it, and help us to come to a better understanding. That's why deities come in pantheons, and that's why we polytheists are inherently suspicious of Gods who claim to hate all other Gods. It's one thing for a God to have an antagonistic relationship with another God—many do—but they should also have Gods who love and befriend them. That's how all things are kept in check and balance.

One could see polytheistic theology as a lot more like the practice of chemistry than monotheistic theology, in that each deity and spirit and force is like a specific element with its own set of properties and behaviors, and each element will combine with other elements in different ways to produce a wide variety of results. Just as with actual chemistry, we humans who live in a world affected by all this continual spiritual combining and reactions must do the work and deductions to figure out what is going on around us, and discern the nature of all those different elements. A monotheistic universe, on the other hand, would be like one composed entirely of hydrogen.

## What You Call Is What You Get: Aspects of the Divine

The ancients understood and agreed that every deity has a variety of aspects, and many of them were specifically named. In Old Norse, they were referred to as *heiti*; some Gods, like Odin, had dozens of them, and some, like Hela, had only one documented aspect. In ancient Greece deities had "surnames" delineating their aspects. (Our modern word for them—epithets—although it has taken on a more blasphemous meaning, comes from the ancient Greek word *epithetos*, meaning "added on".) Aphrodite Genetrix, the aspect of Aphrodite who ruled procreative sex, would interact differently with a worshiper than Aphrodite Porne the patron of whores, or Aphrodite Epitymbidia—Aphrodite on the Tomb, the patroness of everyone who killed themselves or another for love. Yet all were without question Aphrodite.

It's the same for humans, really. The person we are when we are with our beloved in an intimate space is different from the person we are when we're at work, in professional space, or when we are with a group of acquaintances at a strange party. We dress differently, we behave differently, and engage in different activities. The gifts that are appropriate for us to receive will vary depending on whether they come from a co-worker, a lover, a parent, or a child. If any of these people were asked to describe us, nearly all would have an incomplete view and miss important parts of our personal nature. We take this for granted when we're talking about humans, and although we may be surprised to hear that mousy little Mabel skydives as a hobby, we don't vehemently disagree with the truth of the statement, especially when it comes from Mabel's skydiving buddy.

Yet when we apply this to deities, it often seems almost blasphemous to suggest that they have existences as full and complex as ours, with a variety of different faces that they may put on and a variety of ways that they may approach us. It is true that Gods are not humans, and there are significant differences in our natures ... but in this area, we have created too much of a divide in our minds. We see the Gods as static, both in time and in temperament, and unable to change or be different things to different people. It may actually comfort us to see them so, because what is unchanging is always there and always benevolent (or at least acting entirely predictably). It may be that—for at least some of us—this is the fantasy that we've held since childhood of the perfect parent. Many of us don't want to admit that this is the origin of that urge, but in order to get past it, we must acknowledge the power of that infantile desire.

So let's look at the question of divine aspects. I have experienced two categories of aspects, which I casually refer to as "horizontal aspects" and "vertical aspects"—knowing, of course, that this merely two-dimensional approach is a woefully limited description. However, we need words to describe these concepts and communicate about them to each other, even if those words are limited. We must simply make the effort to keep reminding each other that the map is not the territory, and that the Gods work in ways we are not privy to.

### Many Faces, One Being...

"Horizontal" aspects are ones where the difference is in sphere, not distance. Aphrodite Epitymbidia and Aphrodite Porne are both similar in scope; she may only appear as one of those aspects to any given person (or neither; she has many others) but these two "costumes" of hers are not "higher" or "lower" than each other. Similarly, Zeus Teleus who is Hera's bridegroom and Zeus Ctesius the protector of the home, or Apollo Parnopius the bringer of disease and Apollo Iatros the god of physicians, are clearly different but equal "suits" that those Gods wear.

When calling deities by their various epithets, a few patterns have been noted by those whose gifts are such that they have a greater chance of calling them and getting a response. The first pattern is that what you call, you get. As far as we can tell, there are Rules in the cosmos and the Gods must follow them, whether they wish to or not, because those Rules govern their nature and existence. One of these is that if you formally and ritually call a deity with a certain epithet, that's how they'll come, and it does seem to have the ring of a cosmic law to it. Of course, they are not obligated to come at all, and you cannot compel any God to do so—but if they do come, it will be in that form.

There are a few exceptions to this Rule, but they seem to be the exceptions that prove it. Once someone has fully dedicated themselves to a deity (to the point that they have given that deity a good deal of authority over their lives), the deity in question can and will appear in any form they desire, regardless of the wishes of the human being. Full dedication, and the transfer of authority that entails, seems to negate the right to call them through a specific epithet. Another exception, of course, is if the human being knows nothing about epithets and simply calls a God or Goddess by their "main" name; in that case, they cannot complain about the face of the deity that comes. Yet another exception is if the human being calls them with one epithet on their lips and another in their heart (or their subconscious). This may give that deity a choice, or make them more likely to follow words or heart depending on their particular nature.

However it works, this is a power that we have, if we choose to use it. We have it only because it is a natural law, just as they have natural laws that they can use to interact with us. What we call, we get. Of course, we don't always have a handy and complete list of epithets ... and, of course, they are no less powerful, dangerous, or able to affect us just because we call upon a different aspect.

## ...Except When They're Not.

Now that I've made the point about different aspects of the same God, I have to acknowledge that in some religious traditions, that's not the case. In some of the Afro-Caribbean traditions, for example, what an outsider might consider a "god" or "major spirit" with one name and a lot of surnames is actually a number of separate "people" under one spiritual heading. In Vodou, for example, the various aspects of the *lwa* are referred to as "paths", a concept explained by Kenaz Filan, Vodou *houngan si pwen*:

> Within many African Diaspora traditions, there is a concept of *caminos* or "roads" of a particular spirit. Each of these roads is a different way in which the spirit manifests: each may be served using different symbols and offerings and will manifest in a different fashion. Within Lukumi, for example, Obatala Ayagunna will arrive as a brave, sword-wielding warrior: his *eleke* is made with alternating 8 red and 16 white beads. Obatala Ondo is a virgin woman who lives near rocky coasts and protects boats. Each of the orishas may have dozens of these *caminos*. While they will all share some things in common—for example, all Obatalas expect cleanliness and none of them take alcohol—they are definitely different and distinct personalities.
>
> In Vodou these groupings are called "families" or "nations". Within the Ghede *Nachon* (nation) you have the various fun-loving foul-mouthed Ghede who have become famous. There are also spirits like

Baron Kriminel (Baron Assassin; in Kreyol *Kriminel* means murderer, not criminal) who are not at all interested in telling dirty jokes. While they are all considered part of the "root" of the Ghede nation and will all be served with crosses and top-hats, they are not the same individual, as each will quickly inform you should you confuse them. The Nago *Nachon* includes all the spirits named "Ogou". These can range from the old one-legged herbalist Ogou Ossanj to warriors like Ogou Feray and Ogou St. Jacques to skilled tacticians like Ogou Badagris.

If you ask a Houngan or Mambo about this, they will tell you "all Ogous are Ogou". But they will also draw a distinction between the various Ogous, and between the Ogous that manifest on different people during possession. ("Freddy has a powerful Ogou! But you should see Errol's Ogou dancing in the fire when he comes!") Getting more specific answers about this can be very difficult. Vodou is a practical tradition, not one that is greatly concerned with theory or metaphysics. If Ogou comes to you as Ogou St. Jacques, you serve him with the offerings appropriate to St. Jacques: if he comes as Ossanj or Ogou Dessalines—the apotheosis of Haitian revolutionary hero Jean-Jacques Dessalines—you give him those gifts and sing him those songs.

I should also note that these different members of the family are each treated as individuals. There is no idea that the various Ogous are mythic heroes or archetypes: no Vodouisant of my acquaintance believes the Ogous are convenient symbols you can plug into a magic ritual to achieve a desired result. They are considered "mistés" or mysteries, in the Roman Catholic sense. There's an idea that we are not capable of understanding the full depths of these truths or of their relationship with us, Bondye (the Creator) and the world. That doesn't mean that we can't engage with them—indeed, engagement with the mysteries is the whole raison d'être of Vodou. But we cannot expect to understand them or to reduce them to an easily-digested (or even a difficult) set of facts and figures.

I think there's a great deal of wisdom in this approach. Hairsplitting over theological particulars is rarely productive and has frequently led people away from rather than closer to the Divine. That's not to say there is no value in theological speculation or in efforts to gain a better understanding of the Gods. But in the end the theologian has to recognize the limits of reason and even faith. The Gods are immanent in every aspect of our world and touch every aspect of our lives, but that very immanence also means that They will forever be simultaneously within and outside us. We can no more take in every aspect of Their being than a fish can take in every aspect of the ocean.

In a different but similarly frustrating vein, ancient Egyptian deities often blurred together and separated over the centuries, depending on era and area. Sekhmet, Hathor, and Bast were often considered three very different Goddesses with sharply contrasting natures, but then in some times and places one finds the Goddess Sekhmet-Bast, or Sekhmet-Hathor. The God Anpu (known modernly as Anubis) may or may not have also been either of the Gods Wepwawet or Yinepu, who were sometimes worshiped as very separate entities and sometimes as aspects of Anpu ... and in addition, just to confuse the matter, there is a Wepwawet-Yinepu who is his own entity, but not Anpu. With referenced practices like this, it is no wonder that many non-polytheistic scholars roll their eyes at polytheists who insist that Gods are all separate entities. The mystery in this situation is that the Gods are People, but many of them are more fluid in their identities than we are, especially over time. Who is to say that they don't trade around "masks" or aspects, "borrowing" each others' costumes, which happen to come with character names, as needed by the humans of the moment who don't necessarily care about great spiritual truths but just want someone to pray to who symbolizes the right collection of qualities? (This also impinges on the influence that humans can have over Gods, which is a different chapter.) We must also remember that so many of the human names for Gods are variants on "Lord" or "Lady" or "Great One", or simply a term for their job (such as "healer"), that we may well be dealing with multiple deities who have been slapped with one general title by the humans who looked up to them.

In referencing the aforementioned points about the lwa, while we can't know for sure, we might speculate about the also-aforementioned possibility of rare human beings becoming subsumed into Godhead and losing their "self-ness"; might this be the origin of the Vodou "paths" and similar collections of spirits under a single God-name? This is particularly interesting given the fact that Ogou and Obatala, etc., are strictly referred to as "spirits" and not "Gods" in their own tradition. It does seem to contrast with Aphrodite Porne and Aphrodite Epitymbidia, where the aspect-splitting seems to come from within rather from without, but as with all things numinous there probably isn't a strict either-or but a spectrum. We can't be sure of the origin of any aspect unless the spirit in question deigns to tell us.

**Personal To Transpersonal**

"Vertical" aspects of deity are more difficult to describe. For this, I often have to make a little diagram in my head, which I am aware is pitifully inadequate to describe the multifaceted reality of the Divine. However, it helps my mortal meat-brain to get some idea of the concept. Deities have aspects that are more human and less human. We sometimes refer to these as "higher" or "lower" aspects, but the value judgment inherent in those terms makes me reluctant to use them. These aspects are not better or worse than each other; they are solely about how personal and close to human, or how impersonal and close to the undifferentiated divine, an aspect of Deity may be.

Personal aspects—which always get pictured in my head as the little end of a stalactite—are the places where the Gods are closest to human. They argue, they fight, they make mistakes, they are short-sighted and do not access the full truth of their divine abilities. (Although when they err, they do that also on a grand scale.) They also love, with personal fervor as opposed to impersonal distance; they love each other in this way, and sometimes mortals as well.

This is not the kind of love that we think of as in "God loves me," it is a deeply personal and passionate interest in someone, not a transpersonal "Yes, I love your divine spark gently from afar." This is the kind of love offered when a God or Goddess comes to a worshiper and becomes an intimate companion who is always there for you when you need them, offering a shoulder to cry on without judgment for the justice of your pain. The shape of the relationship can still take many forms, which we will discuss in a further chapter, but the key is that you can feel their subjective attention, close up, and you give them yours as well.

As we move up the symbolic stalactite, the aspects become less personal—and less interested in you personally. The higher aspect of a given deity is more emotionally distant, more archetypal, still recognizably *them*, but less human and more godlike. One could imagine it as that deity's "higher self". From the perspective of this aspect, they may still love you, but it is your own higher self that they love, and that love is more impersonal, transpersonal, loving your divine spark rather than your human frailties. From this point, their main interactions with you will have the end-goal of your own self-improvement—bringing you closer to that higher self by any means necessary—and your use in the improvement of the world. From this point, they see high and far and do not make the mistakes that their more human aspects make.

It is hard to describe the qualitative feeling between a humanlike or more godlike aspect of the Divine; it may be one of those many situations common to these interactions where we can only give a frustrating "I know it when I feel it." The quality of the interaction is very different, and the humanlike eye-to-eye intensity is replaced with a sense of overwhelming awe. The gulf between us and them seems much more uncrossable with a higher-self aspect, whereas we are often amazed at how close they seem when they come to us in a humanlike aspect.

## Human Choices

However, there is another Rule that we have found to be true, again and again: You, the mortal, get to choose the vertical aspect in which a deity first appears to you. Moreover, you *do* choose, whether you know it or not. Before God X shows up in your life, God X reaches out to you, and your unconscious—the part of ourselves that we must harness in order to have these experiences—tells them what you want and need. (The unconscious does not lie, as the conscious often does.) They will then appear to you in that aspect, and will continue to make that the main aspect of your dealings with them, unless you consciously choose otherwise. And yes, you can do that as well. If you want, you can consciously choose to interact with a more human or less human aspect, and you don't even have to use an epithet to do that. You can simply ask; they understand your words and your intent. Then you have to pay for whatever you get.

There are gifts and drawbacks to interacting with these different aspects of Deity. The "little" end of a God, the more humanlike side, has a lot of charm for many people. To serve a more human aspect is to bask in the ecstasy of direct emotional attention from a God. It is also this aspect that can make mistakes with people, can overestimate or underestimate them, can lie to them (if it's in that God/dess's inherent nature to do so), and can be less than perfectly ethical with them. This aspect loves them passionately, and gives them personal attention, lays their own prejudices and pettinesses on them, and can be blinded to their long-term Wyrd (although even a deity in a personal relationship with you knows better what you should be doing than any mortal, including yourself; they are still Gods). To choose this is to choose the ecstasy and terror of yielding to the "imperfect" aspect of a deity. It is to love them and be loved by them in a way that those of us who don't have such a relationship cannot even imagine.

It is also to trust them even when you know that they are not acting from their highest selves ... an act of radical spiritual trust. This is the price that they ask for that relationship: that you love them wholly and unconditionally in spite of their flaws and imperfections, and in return they will do the same for you, with an all-consuming love that does not care how messed up you are—and may not attempt to make you any less messed up, because that is the nature of radical acceptance and unconditional love. A deity with whom you have a personal, human-like relationship will put up with a lot more error from you. They will let you wander around and ignore your ideal spiritual path for a much longer time, possibly your whole life ... so long as you love them passionately, in the way that the Hindus refer to as "bhakti". You are expected to be tolerant of their faults, and trust them anyway ... and they will extend that tolerance to you. They will love you passionately no matter how much you continue to screw up, so long as you love them back with equal fervor. You can be petty, and they don't care, because you are giving them the freedom to do the same. While they will endeavor to push you to evolve, it's not the first priority of the relationship. If you can give that deep trust in the face of all else, you can get it reflected back to you with divine intensity, and that is an amazing gift.

On the other side, to serve the higher-self aspect of a Deity is to know that they have your best long-term developmental interest—and the best interest of the world—in the forefront of your dealings with them. It is to know that you can trust them to be Right, to see further than their own desires (and yours) and to act for the greatest good. It is to know that they will never damage you without a reason that is meant for the best long-term outcome, even if it is painful in the moment. You can trust in their unerring judgment with regard to your path and purpose. You can trust that if they send you into the world to work—and with these less human aspects, that is often part of the deal—that they will guide you as part of a vision larger than you can completely comprehend.

As a price, however, they will expect you to also behave as often as possible from the perspective of your higher self, and they will push you toward that place every time you interact with them, both actively (by setting up lessons for you to learn and be improved) and by the pull of their very presence. be pushed hard and mercilessly, and for there to be swift, immediate, and unpleasant consequences when you act in unworthy ways. It's the faster and more spiritually ascetic track, not the track of personal connection. You hold them to their highest standards (and, yes, this is something that we are all allowed to do, regardless of our relationship with them) and in turn they hold you to the highest standards possible given your mortal nature. They will not make mistakes with you, and neither will they surround you with ecstatic love or tell you that you're special. You will be part of their greater purpose, and you will burn off your karmic debts, clean up your personal power, and die a very different person from the one that you began.

This is a choice that we all have, and we are allowed to make and remake that choice again and again. It's something for people who are dissatisfied with the nature of the relationship with their God to think about. You have the power and right to change it, to move it up or down that axis ... if you're willing to pay the price.

Of course, some people deal with different aspects of their Gods, depending on the situation and the deity. You may relate to your "patron" deity, if you have one, in one way, and other Gods in a different way. You may have a personal relationship with one special deity, but sometimes they may switch over to a less human aspect if there is serious work to be done, and its necessity is larger than either of your personal desires. (Where is the consent in that? It occurs because your higher self consents, and deities can talk to that part of you even if you're not consciously listening.) For example, sometimes a divine Spouse can suddenly turn around and be an impersonal Boss for a week or month if it's needed. However, there is generally one aspect/relationship that was chosen first and which both parties revert to ... because it's generally the one that the mortal in question desires and needs the most. Usually there will be some discomfort when there is a temporary shift, and usually it's only done because there is an overriding need having to do with the mortal's well-being. "If I don't get Joe off drugs, he won't be around to have this connection with me any longer."

Why would someone want to choose the "little end" of the divine stalactite, when it requires that dizzying trust in an imperfect but very powerful being? Perhaps because they want and need an aspect of the divine that takes a personal interest in them and their problems. Perhaps because they want an erotic relationship with the Divine, either in order to heal their sexuality, or because relating in that way is part of their spiritual path. Perhaps because they want a love more unconditional than they could ever get from another human being. Perhaps because they need to learn to unconditionally love flawed beings themselves, and starting with a God is a good way to learn that.

Why would someone want to choose a deep, committed relationship with the less human aspect of a deity, when it is impersonal and pushes you constantly to be better, even inflicting painful lessons in order to hurry your process? Perhaps because they need to have a less flawed aspect in order to trust. Perhaps because they crave honorable work and purpose, or want to change the world. Perhaps because their higher self cries out for progress, and they can't seem to move on their own. Perhaps because it is time for them to transform, and they can't do it alone.

A friend of mine who is a priestess and Pagan nun took my stalactite metaphor, clumsy as it is, and went further with it. She pointed out that we humans are the stalagmites, reaching up from the floor of the cave, and sometimes—eventually, in rare cases—we touch the most humanlike end of the divine stalactite that reaches down, and the two join together. In caves, these become pillars of stone from floor to ceiling; in entities, these become Gods with the full understanding of what it is to be human, and also what it is to be undifferentiated-Divine, and every point in between. This suggests the Irminsul, the World-Pillar, the full joining of earth and sky. Perhaps, during our highest moments, we create that pillar if only for a short and ephemeral flutter of time.

We do not always have the choices that we want in our relationship with the Divine. As mystic Caroline Myss says, "God doesn't need your permission to make you live your life." However, we do have some choices, because all interactions are a dance, a balance of some sort. We have choices when we interact with other humans, and with the environment, although not unlimited ones. We have choices, also, when we interact with Gods; we just need to know what they are.

In addition, we need to know why we are making them. Why did you decide to invoke that aspect and avoid that other one? Was the reason clean, or did you have an agenda that serves nothing but your own fears and insecurities? Even if you intend (or hope) to have a personal relationship with a particular deity, ask your higher self about your own motives. If you are hoping, on some level, to get away with something, or even to get away *from* something that you fear, it may not work out the way that you hope. Remember that the Gods can talk to your unconscious, and your higher self, and all the other parts of you. They can also look at your destiny and the thread in the greater pattern that is you, and may make a decision based less on your desires and more on the whole of what needs to happen. Sometimes the Universe—above both you and the distinct aspects of the Gods—outvotes everyone, and it always wins. In the next chapter, we'll talk about going still further up that stalactite, and what happens then.

## Going Higher: Immanence and Transcendence

After all the discussing I've done so far about polytheism and the separateness of deities, now I have to talk about when the situation isn't so clear. What happens when we follow the nature of deity upward past their less humanlike aspect?

What happens is that the Gods do, on that level, begin to blend together. They seem to blend by affinity—love goddesses together, death gods together—and yet they are more complex than that, so their blendings do not resemble our simplistic two-dimensional ideas about them. However, please keep in mind that at this level their interactions with human beings are extremely transpersonal, which means, also, impersonal. They are less likely to love you in a focused, individual way, and more likely to extend love toward your higher self, drawing it out instead of your emotions. They are also less likely to make contact with you in general.

Above this is what could be called the Architect of the Universe, although even to say that would imply more of a human consciousness than is actually there. We, with our meat-brains and mortal lives, have a terrible time conceiving of anything we can't anthropomorphize in some way, and that includes the "highest"—or most transpersonal, anyway—level of Existence. This is not about some divine Father or Mother who is set over the other Gods. This is about their higher selves blending together, and the point just beyond that. It both is and is not separate from them and from us. Is that confusing? Of course it is. The further we get from humanness, the further we get from anything we can conceive of in human terms.

So let's leave human terms, and stick to observations. The observed fact, in my experience, is that to the Architect of the Universe, we are motes of dust, and we get the attention given to motes of dust. The problem is that human beings often love the idea of getting personal attention from the Highest Form Of Existence, because our ego thinks that would be the best sort of attention—ironically, given that all the oldest transcendent religions have observed that the only way to get any closer to the Architect of the Universe is to give up ego entirely, as well as the need to get personal attention and all the rest of our human foibles. It's the paradox of transcendence—the only way to get to the top of the mountain is to eventually lose all your reasons for getting there. That road, viewed in an ego-based and judgmental manner, can be a way of denigrating the personal-god experience as a "lesser" one, a mistake which we as polytheists must not allow ourselves to make.

## This Terrible, Beautiful World

This brings us to one of the underlying questions: is this life, this incarnation in flesh and the material world, a prison or a privilege? Our worldview as polytheists, and especially as animists, is the latter. We were not sent here to make our life's work a mad scramble to get out. I've always found wry humor in the fact that transcendent religions whose main push is escape from this mortal coil have to put in some kind of an anti-suicide clause to keep people from jumping to the obvious conclusion. Simply stepping willfully off the wheel has to have negative consequences—you spend eternity in a bad place, or you just come back again with a worse situation—because there is no other way to lock someone into disliking this world enough to sacrifice anything to leave it ... the hard way. In order to keep someone on that narrow one-size-fits-all path, you need to create a punishment for choosing what might look like the logically simple answer—which, to the transcendent-leaning mind, is cheating.

As someone who does believe in reincarnation—although not necessarily for everyone, and we'll get to that when we discuss death—I'm not saying that suicide never ends with someone coming back and facing challenges that they never got through the last time, but it is not a punitive situation. When you throw a ball into the air, misjudge your aim, and it falls in your face, that's not a punishment. It's just cause-and-effect; it's not personal. All too often we make the mistake of believing that situations are personal when they aren't, and then decide that "shit happens" when it's uncomfortable to notice the chain of effects from our own actions. But more on that conundrum later in the book.

It's not always difficult to believe that this material world is a terrible place where we are imprisoned and destined to suffer. Disease, cruelty, violence, famine, and natural disasters can make this world a very unpleasant place at times—but it is still a privilege to be here. This is one of my basic underlying understandings of the immanent Pagan world view, as opposed to the transcendent-religion view. My faith only makes sense when viewed on top of this bedrock of certainty: we are here because we are meant to experience here fully, not because we are supposed to get away quickly. The more fully we experience it, the more we learn, and the better equipped we are for our spiritual evolution.

That doesn't mean that we have to do everything in one lifetime, but it does mean: Be Here Now. Find value in Here.

From this root we follow the branch of the tree: If Here is just as valuable and sacred as any other place, and if the material forms we take are just as valuable and sacred as any other less material form—*and if we really believe that*—then the quest to make the furthest and least human form of the Divine take notice of us and make us its special pet shows itself to be the world-hating, body-hating, nature-hating, and human-nature-hating attitude that it all too often is. To say that the person whose most beloved forms of divinity are the lake-spirit and forest-spirit behind their house is some sort of superstitious spiritual underachiever denigrates the wisdom and power of the natural world we are meant to experience. To say that someone whose interactions are only humanlike personal relationships with the most human forms of the Divine is less evolved than someone whose relationship is a vague and impersonal one with a much less humanly defined God denigrates the human path that we are meant to tread, and the amazing generosity of the Gods and spirits who are willing to come partway down to our level in order to interact with us, to the joy of both parties.

This point brings us back around to the issue discussed in the last chapter, which is the problem of honoring Gods who are imperfect and less than omnipotent. As we mentioned, it's not unusual for these qualities to be used as reasons why people reject dealing with separated forms of divinity and chase after the Big Undifferentiated, hoping this is will differentiate enough to notice them. There is a way to connect, at least to some extent, with that huge and impersonally loving power, but to be a polytheist is to take a different route. Just as we had to recreate an adult relationship with our parents once we became adults, so polytheism demands an adult approach to divinity. Unlike our parents, this does not mean that we are their equals. It does mean, however, that we must acknowledge their emotions and preferences and agency beyond simply taking care of us, besides simply filling the one us-centered role that we like to see them in. Once we were adults, we had to understand that our parents may have been people with actual adult passions, including physical sexual desires. Difficult as that may have been for us to wrap our heads around, we needed to understand that if we were going to understand them fully as whole people. Perhaps some of us didn't care about seeing them as whole people, and preferred our truncated version. Perhaps some of us feel that way about the

Gods as well ... and the only problem with that is when the Gods decide to teach you different, whether you like it or not.

Some people, of course, are meant to work with the pantheistic/panentheistic aspects of Deity, and struggle with that impersonal faraway voice, just as some are meant to work with the smaller and more humanlike aspects of Deity. Neither choice is better than the other, any more than the mountain goat is more evolved than the prairie-dwelling buffalo. It's we humans, with our short-sightedness, who make every binary into another form of Good/Bad. However, the temptation to take the transcendental path uncleanly—meaning to take it with any remaining vestige of assumption that it is an inherently superior path—is huge and overwhelming. It will be a very special individual who can walk it without that poison seeping in. As I am not on a transcendental path, I cannot say if there is or is not a way to get Up There while still carrying that baggage, but knowing what I know about the Universe and its desire for our personal evolution, I'd bet against it in any wager.

## Binary Ambivalences

At this point, I have to talk about binaries, and I have to apologize for having used terms like "higher" and "lower" to discuss the nature of the Gods. We are impoverished when it comes to language for talking about these concepts; so many of our terms have connotations that lead us back into the very world-hating attitude that we are trying desperately to scramble out of in the first place. When I refer to the impersonal aspects of the Gods as "higher" and the personal aspects as "lower", I am aware that for many people, this will automatically be overlaid with another binary, the one labeled Good/Bad, or Desirable/Undesirable. We humans do this, over and over; it's one of our most crippling flaws. It's not just found in more modern cultures either; even ones that do not have their very deities enacting that binary literally do have aspects of that very human flaw in their cultural customs (especially around In The Tribe/Not In The Tribe and similar situations). Somehow, whenever we see a binary, we automatically try to decide which side has more intrinsic value (thereby lessening the value of the other one), perhaps so we will have some scale on which to choose for ourselves. It's not easy to choose from a place of "What will be right for me personally?" If we don't have a sense of that yet, we revert to attempts to find intrinsic value even when it's slightly ridiculous.

Sunrise/sunset. Summer/winter. Dark/light. Up/down. Male/female. I could go on, but these are easy examples of binary pairs we have imbued with arbitrary Good/Bad connotations. Looked at objectively, there is no such judgment, and that is the view we need to take if we are to fully live this immanent Pagan life. Even binaries like yin/yang, which were created in a system that was originally meant to show that both sides were sacred, eventually gained a value judgment. (You don't think so? Poll twenty random people as to which they think makes up more of their nature, and *listen to their tone of voice when they answer*.)

I don't believe that we need to throw out binaries, as some would suggest. Binaries are sacred things as well, perfect opposites in eternal balance of beauty and harmony. Even when they oppose each other, they can often see things in the other that the other does not see, and that kind of perspective is needed. Both sides of every binary are valuable. Instead of eliminating them, I believe that we need to make a personal discipline of excising the habit of laying a Good/Bad binary over them, and consciously preventing ourselves from doing it when faced with all the binaries in our life.

Here's the exercise: Say "higher Gods" and "lower Gods". Right now, say those words. Did your mind put a desirable/less desirable connotation on them? That's what you need to work on. How can you change your thinking so that you can say those words aloud, and they will be full of meaning and image but will be entirely without that connotation?

The first step to do this is to bombard your mind with alternative images. Does "down" always have to be bad? When is it just as beautiful as up, or more so? What's the danger in being "high", in every sense? Now, in your mind see them both as their best possible connotation together, at the same time. Now see them together as their worst connotation, at the same time. From this point on, don't ever let yourself see one as good and the other as merely problematic. Insert a mental footnote, a tripwire to reroute your thoughts and concentrate them on the two points of the binary in perfectly opposed harmony, both equally valuable (or problematic, if it works better that way for you). Work on that. When you get it right with this binary, pick another one and keep going.

Part of why this is important is that there's a deeper truth we must fully understand: every binary is actually a spectrum. We know this, although we don't always talk about it, and part of why we ignore it is the overlaid judgmental binary. When one end is Valued and the other end is Devalued, our emotional responses to observing the spectrum of liminal points in between becomes much more emotionally volatile. We have to decide, perhaps unconsciously, where the point of value stops. If "light" is good and "dark" is bad, at what point does a shade in between become negative? You can bet that humans have already had huge arguments over that point, when it's really so irrelevant. If you remove the value judgment from the binary, it becomes much easier to switch from binary to spectrum and back again without a negative emotional reaction. As someone who was born both male and female, it's crucially important to me that we as human beings learn to do this, as soon as possible, one human being at a time if necessary.

So from here, let's reexamine the title of this chapter: Going Higher. Without a value judgment, that simply means moving into the realm where the Gods begin to blur and become less distinct, less human, less involved in our world, and less interested in us personally. While some people are called to work largely with these aspects—and perhaps with the point where they blur altogether—it is not the calling for everyone, or even most people. It doesn't make one more evolved, either. It may just be about balance. Perhaps those who are legitimately called to a pantheistic, panentheistic, or even higher henotheistic relationship with the Gods are the people who tend to cut things up into little pieces too often, to refuse to see the forest for the trees, to concentrate on petty details instead of looking at the big picture. Perhaps those who are called to work with more specific aspects are the people who think big and vague, and forget their own humanness. Perhaps there are a multitude of reasons more subtle and personal than this, but each aimed at making someone more evolved through their relationship to the Gods. Because even at their most human and faulty end, they still see and know more than we do. Trust me on that point. Better yet, trust them.

## Not Quite Divine: Spirits, Ancestors, and Animism

It is said that the first religion was ancestor worship, and that our connection with the Gods came later. To this day, ancestors are honored, blessed, ritually redeemed, and propitiated in a number of polytheistic faiths around the world and in Neo-Paganism. In addition, some groups honor and propitiate—in other words, find worthy of *worthship*—spirits of the land, plants, animals, and other areas of life. To say, "You are wonderful," or "I ask for your help," or "I ask you to look well upon me, because I know that your good wish has power," can be construed as worship, but it does not mean that you believe they are Gods, only that they are worthy and have powers beyond your own. Reverence for unseen beloved entities is not limited to Gods, although if the monotheistic mindset is bewildered by giving one's reverence to more than the Highest Of High Gods, it is even more bewildered by the idea of giving it to entities which one does not even really consider deities. In spite of this, the world is teeming with spirits who call out for relationship with us, whether we can see or hear it or not. Some of these include:

- ❖ **Ancestors.** When one thinks of ancestors, one generally thinks first of one's blood kin, and that's the most basic definition of ancestral spirits. However, there are other sorts of ancestors as well. There are ancestors of the mind and spirit—people who inspired you with their writing or their courage or by demonstrating other laudable qualities, and it is perfectly acceptable to honor them as ancestors for their deeds. If you are in an order, cult, denomination, craft, or trade with a lineage that is passed down, you can honor the people in that line of knowledge-descent as your lineage-ancestors. If you belong to a particular demographic of people who have always been around to one extent or another, and whose experience in the world is so unique that it extends across the years and defines you (and possibly them) much more than your family ever could, they can also be honored and called upon as ancestors.

- ❖ **Land-spirits.** The ancient Romans had the concept of *genus loci,* the spirits of place. In Norse and Germanic traditions, there are the *landvaettir*, or *landwights*. Celtic traditions speak of the "little folk" who are more earth-spirit than elves, and Shinto has its *kami* in every stone, every tree, every blade of grass. Each specific area of land has its own land-spirit—including cities, which generally have a city-spirit instead. The indwelling land-spirit wears the soil and bedrock and other matter like a body. It is aware of everything that happens on its piece of earth—or could be, if it cared; some land-spirits choose to ignore certain things, finding them unimportant, and some are semi-permanently hibernating. Some will gladly latch onto humans who make contact with them, and some will ignore humans entirely. As most modern people will not live and die on the same piece of land, our dealings with land-spirits are often temporary and ephemeral, and this does seem to sadden the ones who like to communicate with humans, as they are much older than we are and take a longer view of things. Allying yourself with land-spirits through love, intent, and propitiation can help keep you safe on your property, alert you to intruders, grow your garden taller, and give you the chance at experiencing a true oneness with the Earth. On a smaller scale, I could include the spirits of old buildings, and house spirits. The latter have come under many names, from the Roman Lares to the Celtic brownie, but are basically benevolent spirits which choose to guard and care for a home and all the people in it ... so long as they are acknowledged and honored in some way.

❖ **Elemental Spirits.** Earth, water, air, fire—these are the basic "elements" in Neo-Paganism. They could also be translated as solids, liquids, gas, and energy—the basic forms of Nature. We attribute a variety of corresponding qualities to them in Neo-Pagan theory, which they symbolize in most of our denominations. Most of those elemental affinities were assumed from observing our interactions with elemental spirits. Elementals have short attention spans and are further removed from humanity than Gods or other more humanlike spirits; their natures are simpler, although they are not stupid. They come in many forms—water-spirits, for example, might be lake-spirits, river-spirits, bog-spirits, or ocean spirits. Some are very small and short-lived, and some are so large and powerful that they can be considered Gods to an extent.

Some are kin to land-spirits (and indeed some would class many types of land-spirits as a form of earth-elemental) and have been propitiated by those local to their physical "body", and wanting their blessing. One example of this would be the Roman river-god Tiberis, who was worshiped and propitiated as a local deity by those living within his purview. Others might be the Gods of Lake Baikal, the largest inland body of water which has always been considered sacred to those living around it, or Pele the Hawaiian goddess of the Kilauea volcano, or Lady Ganga, the goddess of the sacred river of India. Maintaining relationships with elemental spirits helps one to understand that element deeply, and to gain aid in problems deriving both from the natural workings of that element and from its associated qualities. (For example, a fire-spirit could help speed your metabolism, protect your house from flame, and help you to find courage.)

❖ **Plant and Animal Spirits.** Here I must differentiate between the life force and personality of a specific plant or animal—that dog, that fly, that oak tree or clump of plantain—and the great overarching spirit of each species—Grandfather Wolf or Grandmother Mugwort. These very old and wise spirits have been referred to as "devas", and the powers of the most popular ones have been recounted in myths and folktales (such as the "Elder-Mother" of Hans Christian Andersen's story). If they choose to be in relationship with you, they can help with many problems from physical health to spiritual wisdom. They usually have relationships with the Gods themselves as well, and can "broker" a connection in that way. It is also important to remember that some animal and plant Grandparents chose to link themselves wholly with humanity and nourish them—partly out of self-interest, but mostly out of love. These are the common livestock and food-plant species, the Ancestral Fathers and Mothers as they are called in my tradition, and we are still dependent on that relationship today, even if we are in partial violation of the contract due to harmful agricultural practices. Actually, many people who work with plant and animal spirits find that the offerings they expect most often are not items, but actions. They may require that you become more mindful about what you eat and how you treat the Earth, and modify your actions accordingly. They generally have no trouble with humans eating animals and plants, because that's part of the natural order, but they require kindness and respect in our food-producing practices.

- ❖ **Demigods and Almost-Gods.** These can include the not-as-powerful relatives and servants of the Gods, who nonetheless do have great power and wisdom, and are worthy of reverence. However, with this category we are getting, again, into the slippery question of what is a God and what is not. The honest truth is that there is no way to draw that line cleanly. There are beings that I am sure are divine, and there are beings that I am sure are not, and there is a frustratingly large grey area in between. Generally, I use the word "spirit" as an umbrella term for any sort of non-corporeal being, from a deity on downwards. Many of the casual Pagan definitions of "God" and "Not-God" have more to do with who the people in question prefer to worship than any thoughtful usage. All too often, "Gods" are who the speaker worships, and "Not-Gods" are who they don't. I choose not to try to draw that line, and I generally go with the words of a friend of mine: "If it's bigger, older, and wiser than I'll ever be, then I treat it as a God and go from there."

## Yes, Really, It's All Alive

This brings us in turn to the question of animism, another term that we touched on in the Definitions chapter. While not all polytheistic faiths are also animist, a great number—probably the majority—most certainly are. All the ancient polytheistic religions acknowledged a wide variety of spirits indwelling in the natural world, and most included the indwelling spirits of Nature in their pantheons to one extent or another, regardless of how later scholars divided it up. In an animistic worldview, everything in nature is alive—not just plants and animals, but bodies of water, stones, mountains, the dirt itself. Many man-made objects are also alive. In ancient times, every lasting man-made object was a product of many hours of concentrated work, and became alive through attention, focus, and the directed energy of its making. Today, objects made in a similar way can also develop souls and life-energy, although they may or may not need human attention to keep that soul in them. However, the ancients did not have mass-produced items, most of which do not seem to contain life force per se; therefore it probably never occurred to them that humans could make something at such a remove that it would have none of their attention, and never become ensouled.

And yet, plastic trash aside, the rest of the world is still alive. An animist viewpoint gives one a different perspective on the world. Of course, one can still understand fully that the world is alive, and that all things in it are interconnected parts of life, and still not love the natural world or care about it. While many of the ancient written records we have about early western religion put a great deal of effort into propitiating spirits of land and nature, many of the later pre-Christian forms were urban in nature, and reflected the struggle of civilization against nature (which, at that time, did have the upper hand) and the most-loved Gods were those who upheld civilization, not those who privileged wildness and natural processes. The ancients did struggle with this dichotomy, even as we do, but we struggle with it from a point where civilization seems to be dealing Nature some fatal blows. In our case, as the world has shifted, so must we shift and look at our spiritual relationship with Nature, and not only its Gods but its indwelling spirits as well.

Certainly the Gods and spirits of nature have been reaching out to human beings on a greater scale in the past half-century or so; I do not believe that our "sudden" growing interest in various forms of natural spirits, after centuries of mostly disparaging them, is accidental. It seems possible that they themselves have been reaching out in self-defense, trying to bring us back into a healthier balance before we make too many irrevocable mistakes. Even more than a polytheistic worldview, an animistic worldview does lend itself well to learning to love and protect the life that one sees all around, and to understand one's self as an inextricable part of the web of life, which can be shaken and damaged by our blind thrashing about.

In a fully animist worldview, we would consider it beneficial to discuss all major decisions with the spirits of the plants, animals, and places before making major changes to them. Serious genetic transformations would be discussed through communion with the Grandfather and Grandmother spirits of the plant and animal species involved. The keeping of livestock would be in harmony with the original contract of sacrifice and respect that we made with their spirit-ancestors, as would the treatment of the food plants who we consider our Ancestral Fathers and Mothers, whose destiny is entwined with ours. Before building anything, or mining, or otherwise drastically developing land, we would have to discuss things with the land-spirit who we were planning to disturb; urban planning would be best done with an eye to the opinion of the city-spirit. Substances removed from the bowels of the earth would be replaced with some kind of acceptable offering, determined by negotiation with the earth-spirits. Waterway-spirits would be consulted before being dammed or diverted, and the ocean spirits would certainly have opinions worth reckoning. The Gods could be seen as intermediaries in this work, speaking for both sides in turn depending on their alliances and specialties.

While this will sound to many like a fantasy world, something that can never happen, it's certainly achievable in tiny ways in one's own life, and after all, that is where change starts—small moves. Start with the food you eat, the animals you keep (even as pets), the medications you take (if they are plant or animal-derived), the land that you live on (or the city-spirit). There are plenty of books out there with details on how to begin this process, but I believe it would be good for all Pagans to spend at least a short time living inside this worldview, just for the sake of education. It drives home, on a visceral level, just how interconnected we really are.

## Being In Relationship: The Human-Divine Exchange

Just as each person that we meet is going to choose a different sort of relationship with us, so each deity who chooses to connect with us will decide on what sort of relationship they want with each of us, and no two will be the same. This includes the same deity interacting with different people, and even the same deity interacting with two people who hold a similar position with them. The Gods are not stupid, I tell people continually. When a God/dess chooses to put out the energy to connect with you, they know what kind of relationship will be most mutually fulfilling to both parties.

A few deities may, admittedly, lean a little toward either your fulfillment or theirs, and which way they lean will have more to do with their intrinsic nature than anything else. However, a God/dess will be far more aware than you are of the necessary balance in all things, a balance that is the mainspring of the Universe and that will come back around. The laws of consequence work for everything, including deities, and they know this better than we do. They will not unbalance the scales of relationship unless they intend to rebalance them again in some way further down the road. It's all an ongoing exchange of energy, and they can often see better than we can when it comes to balancing it with the best long-term result.

Of course, since we humans tend to live in the short term, it can sometimes seem a bit unfair. That's where trust comes in. Trusting a deity to have your long-term best interests in mind can be a terribly difficult thing. Even trusting the Universe in general to do so can be excruciatingly hard. I know that for myself, believing in the reality of the Gods was never hard. Believing in their benevolence toward me has always been the harder lesson, especially when I have been pushed by those divine hands into doing things that were painful and caused me to suffer. However, over time I realized that everything I was forced by them to do or experience turned out to be the right road in the long run. This was in contrast to the decisions I made for myself, which had a much higher chance of being wrong. If I learned to trust the Gods, it was because I saw their track record. This could only have been learned over time, and I don't feel that there was any shame in needing to see evidence of that greater purpose. For myself, once I could know something of that purpose, I could throw myself more fully behind it. For others, however, having faith in the absence of evidence may be their lesson.

## Chains of Command

As we discussed in prior chapters, the closer a deity's aspect is to our level of existence—and the closer a "smaller-than-a-deity" spirit is to our level of existence—the less likely they are to be able to fully see that long-range balance and to naturally flow with it. As we also discussed, one can always call upon the higher aspect of a deity—and, similarly, one can call upon the "spiritual superior" of a smaller spirit. The spirit of that oak tree is subject to the wisdom of Grandfather Oak, the overarching spirit of that species of tree. Grandfather Oak is subject to the wisdom of a higher, much more impersonal power that I can only call the Green One, the spirit of all plants. We have honored that spirit as the Green Man in ancient times—little more than a personification for most of us, because most humans cannot fully attune to a deity who really has no human aspect—but some see that deity as the Green Mother.

Similarly, the spirit of that dog is subject to the wisdom of the Great Dog Spirit, who is subject to the wisdom of the Lord or Lady of Animals. We are genetically a little closer to animals than to plants, so the Lord or Lady of Animals shares some essence with the higher aspects of some of our Gods—Herne, Diana, etc. The point of all this is that you always have the option of taking an issue with a particular spirit (or even a deity) to a higher court, as it were—but do keep in mind that the higher you call, the less likely the spirit will be to humor your human-convenience-centered perspective, and may require a great deal of widening of that perspective before they will consider assisting you.

## Diversity In Everything, Including Relationships

When people first get into polytheistic Pagan religion and start looking at the array of Gods before them, their first thought is to look for the deities who are more immediately attractive to them. Often they are desperate to get into a "patron deity" relationship, with an urgency that reminds me uncannily of the social pressure to get one's self into a monogamous marriage as quickly as possible. Some people, of course, are dedicated to a particular deity to one extent or another, occasionally even to the point of henotheism, but the majority of polytheists are not so monogamous in their spirituality—and neither do the Gods ask that of most people.

Not everyone has a "patron deity", as I tell the hundreds of supposed polytheists every year who message me and ask, "How do I choose a patron deity?" When I question them as to why this is a need for them, all too many of them are coming from an unconsciously monotheistic view. While they do believe in the existence and holiness of a variety of Gods, on some level they feel that they need to pick one who is "more special" than all the rest, and focus on that one ... because that's the model they know. Many of them seem to yearn for henotheism as the "next best thing" to monotheism, because the idea of having loving and devoted relationships with a variety of Gods seems almost adulterous—almost unfaithful—to the One that they haven't even found yet. While some people do devote the majority of their devotion to one God of many—they have "patron deities", to one extent or another—all the ones I know who walk that path tell me that they were very specifically chosen by that God/dess, in ways that could not be denied. On the other hand, many—or even most—polytheists are not meant to walk that path. Instead, they are given free choice as to whom to dedicate what percentage of their energy. They may choose on the basis of activity-affinity ("I raise goats, Thor likes goats, I'll venerate Thor!") or personality affinity ("I can really relate to the struggles of Inanna, I'm so like that myself...") or they may dedicate themselves to a specific deity for a determined length of time, and then explore a different divine path as it arises.

Instead, the array of deities is matched by an array of relationship possibilities just as diverse. (Do not forget that diversity is sacred to polytheistic, earth-centered religion. Remind yourself of this, again and again, and think hard about the real implications of that view.) Relationships with deities depend on two qualities: chosen style, and level of connection. The first—the style of the relationship—is chosen mutually by both the deity and the human being. If there is a disagreement, the deity is going to win, because the human being cannot force the deity to enter into a specific relationship style, and the deity always has the option of cutting the connection entirely. They can always say No, and in most cases the human being can say No as well. (We'll discuss the exceptions further on.)

The second quality is the level of connection—the ability to communicate with each other—that each person may have with their deity. As we've mentioned previously, one of the general beliefs in the modern Pagan demographic is the idea that everyone is born with the capacity to connect psychically with Gods, spirits, the higher Universe, etc. and that it is only repressive societies (and perhaps families) who prevent everyone from being a psychic dynamo. This is in stark contrast to the beliefs of Hinduism and other eastern religions, who believe that everyone is born closed-up and psychic connections must be gained through years of hard work at proven techniques. (It is in even starker contrast, and was probably generated as a reaction against, the general view of the Abrahamic religions, which is that natural connection is a great rarity granted only to occasional saintly types, and limited connection can only be granted to priests by organizational fiat.)

In my experience, certain rarer styles of relationship require a high level of two-way communication between human and deity or human and spirit, but that connection is not necessarily a sign of a greater level of devotion, or being more evolved as a person. Nor, in my experience, are the gifts of natural connection distributed evenly among the human race, unfortunately. General observation seems to show that it is more likely that they run in families and skip generations, which would make them genetically based in an incredibly unfair distribution. While the great work of developing and improving one's signal clarity is beyond the scope of this small book (and we are working on putting one out that will cover it), I can certainly verify that no one ever failed to hear the voices of the Gods and spirits because they were an unworthy human being. Such variables as distraction, lack of focus, low innate ability, fear, grief, poor diet, poor health, high chemical load, or general disbelief can all get in the way, but it has nothing to do with one's worth as a person. A worshiper who never hears the Gods that they devoutly worship may well be one of their favorites, and the Gods may bless their life accordingly. Nor does the chosen role indicate worth as a human being; people in every one of these roles will have flaws, problems, and room for improvement. With that as a given, let's look at a list of the different types of human-deity relationships.

- ❖ **None At All:** Does not believe in the existence of the Gods.

- ❖ **Novice:** Is beginning to believe in and learn about the Gods, but does not yet have enough information to be drawn to any specific ones.

## Dealing With Deities

❖ **Worshiper:** Believes in the Gods and worships them in group ritual, or occasionally on their own when moved to do so. Some might pray, but hear nothing back. Others might hear something occasionally, but not often, nor all that strongly. Is not bound to any one deity, and they are a "layman" in their religious practice rather than holding a priestly role. Is not required to belong to a religious group.

❖ **Devotee:** Has one or a handful of deities with whom they have a special relationship. The relationship is entirely personal; any communication between human and Divine is for the benefit of that person and their spiritual path. Some do not have two-way communication with their patron deit(ies), but simply love them with sincere emotion. Others speak to them regularly and are answered, at least some of the time. Is not required to belong to a religious group.

❖ **Clergyperson:** Is in service to a religious community as part of their service to the Gods. For instance, in my church, we differentiate between *priests/priestesses* (clergy whose job is to run ritual, hold services for, teach about, or do the sacred work of specific Gods, such as a "priestess of Artemis" who would do all those things in service to her goddess); and *ministers*, who serve the community more widely, with the sort of service tasks and activities expected of most mainstream Abrahamic-religion clergypeople—counseling, organizing, aiding the unfortunate, running rituals/services, marrying, burying, etc. One can be both a priest and a minister in this model, of course, and many are. Being a priest/ess of a particular deity is likely to involve at least a little human/divine contact, but being a minister requires nothing but religious devotion and a commitment to the community.

❖ **Spirit-worker:** Has been chosen by the Gods to be in a *working* relationship with them, in order to do a specific job for the community. In most cases this is a service job which involves helping clients through a specific traditional spiritual practice, but occasionally it can be about service to a holy site, temple, or other spiritual duty. The roles of "shaman" and "shamanic practitioner" are subsets of this role. Some spirit-workers are also clergy;

some are not. Requires a high level of human/divine communication, by the very nature of the job.

- **Mystic:** Has made a deep spiritual commitment to devote their lives to a particular deity or set of deities. While some mystics are also clergy or spirit-workers, for many it is only about a personal spiritual devotion that fills and influences their whole lives. Being a mystic usually involves a high level of human/divine connection, as the continual striving for that connection is part of the path.

- **God-servant:** Has chosen to dedicate themselves to serving one specific deity (or, sometimes, a small number of them), usually to do the work that their patron values most in the world. This relationship has negotiated boundaries, and can be short-term or lifelong depending on what both parties agree to. A god-servant might be a priest, or spirit-worker, or mystic, or none of those things. The modern term among Northern Tradition Pagan practitioners is *godathegn*.

- **God-slave:** Has been chosen by the Gods—sometimes without their consent—to serve them in whatever capacity the Gods deem most useful, with the entirety of their lives. Is generally lifelong and permanent. Very rare, as it is karmically expensive to reroute a human being's entire destiny and free will, even for Gods; this generally only happens when there is dire necessity, and enough karmic debt in someone's past to make them "affordable" to the deity that buys them up. A god-servant may become a god-slave if they agree to it. A god-slave may be a spirit-worker or clergyperson, but generally has a spiritual "job" of some kind, as the "dire necessity" is generally about other humans who need help. Many, though not all, Pagan shamans are god-slaves. Being a god-slave requires a high level of human/divine communication. The modern term among Northern Tradition Pagan practitioners is *godatheow*; some Hellenics use the ancient Cretan word *doera* to describe this concept.

- **God-spouse:** Has been chosen by a deity as a wife or husband, and has agreed to it. Considers themselves to be married to that deity, and lives their life in a way that expresses this experience. Levels of human/divine connection vary, but a very strong devotional relationship is necessary. A god-spouse may also be clergy (especially as a priest/ess of their deity), a spirit-worker, a mystic, a god-servant or god-slave, or simply a very serious devotee. Marriage to a deity is usually for life; those few who have obtained "divorces" generally did it by appealing to a deity who had some kind of authority over their divine spouse. (As an aside, people in other roles may have sexual relations with one or more deities, especially if they have a high human/divine connection, but those relationships do not necessarily become permanent marital bonds. Some simply remain occasional ritual lovers.)

- **God-child:** Just as some people have strong romantic and marital attachments to their patron deity, others feel themselves to be in a parent-child relationship with them. There is often a feeling of having been "created" by them, perhaps through that deity manipulating their early life circumstances to achieve a certain effect, or even having manipulated their family line. Some feel that they have the "blood", or genetic heritage, of that deity, and have inherited some of their traits or that of their divine family. Others simply feel as if their deity has "adopted" them. This role may be combined with any of these other roles, or none; it may have any level of human/divine connection.

- **Horse:** Allows deities to "borrow" their body for ceremonial/religious purposes, usually during a ritual. (This is more the description of a job than a relationship, but since it does affect the interactions between human and divine, I'll list it here anyhow. Some Pagan groups practice spirit-possession or God-possession; some do not.) No "horse" can "carry" every deity; usually there is a question of psychological and spiritual affinity, and the Gods decide who is an acceptable vehicle for them. The horse is usually a priest/ess, spirit-worker, mystic, god-servant, or god-slave. Fairly rare, as it requires specific neurology, and requires a high level of human/divine connection. (For more information on the phenomenon of God-possession in the Pagan demographic, refer to the book I co-authored with Kenaz Filan, *Drawing Down The Spirits*, available through Inner Traditions Press.)

- ❖ **Embodiment:** A very rare relationship, this is a devotee with a very strong human/divine connection whose personality has become so congruent with that of their God/dess that they come to embody much of that deity's traits, and become a walking source of that deity's energy. They may or may not have any of the other roles, in addition.

- ❖ **Avatar:** The rarest relationship of all. This involves a deity actually taking a small piece of their own soul and allowing it to incarnate in a human body. According to ancient accounts of various religions, avatars are generally aware of their nature from the beginning, and immediately go about the business of the deity of whom they are a small part.

One of the differences between Paganism and some other religions is that most of the roles given above are purely subjective in nature. One takes on a role because one is called to it, not because one is granted the role by a human religious authority. The major exception is that of clergy; many Pagan groups, churches, and denominations have their own training programs for clergypeople. The role of priest or priestess may be one granted by a group, or may be begun by a solitary person as a devotional activity, but it usually turns, one way or another, into a community job. Being a shaman or shamanic practitioner starts with being chosen by or drawn to specific Gods and spirits, but in order to wear the title from a specific tradition one must study under an elder practitioner in that tradition. In addition, anyone can declare themselves a horse, but they will generally not be accepted to practice in a group ritual unless that group has observed them and believes their claim, or they have very good references from some other group. However, the rest of the roles are a matter of the personal relationship between a human being and their Gods, and no earthly authority can bestow or withdraw them.

## Trusting Both Gods And Self

Each human/divine relationship is different, with many subtle nuances, just as every human/human relationship is different. Each one of the above roles can also be joined with any aspect of a deity, including more human and less human ones. No one should feel badly because their relationship with their God(s) does not resemble that of the person next to them—it's virtually impossible for it to be so. The Gods know what is right for each of us, better than we do; at the very least, they have access to that information about us once they are in relationship. Who and what we are to each other is between us, and us alone. Rather than listening to the words of others on what we should be to the Gods, we should be working harder to become people who can more clearly and cleanly connect with them, and thus be in better relationship. The principle is the same with non-divine spirits, although they cannot necessarily be expected to know the fullness of our destinies, and allowances must be made for that. Still, they can see clearly enough to notice qualities about us that we might not see in ourselves.

The subjectivity of the problem gives rise to another question: At what point is the spirit powerful and knowledgeable enough that I must obey them? That's a question with many layers of answer which must be peeled away. First, what is your relationship to the deity in question? Do they have a long-standing connection with you? Have you loved them for a long time, and have you felt their love in return, if only obliquely? In a relationship such as this, they are more likely to know you thoroughly—including not only your heart and soul but your destiny as well—and to work for your best interest. If this is the first time that a deity has spoken to you, be sure that they are really who they say they are. There are, unfortunately, a number of lesser spirits out there who will claim to be Deity X—or anyone, really—if they think that they can get some energy out of it. Ideally, someone who works closely with that deity—and even more ideally, one who doesn't know you well—should pray for a message and validate for you that indeed, it was their God/dess who spoke to you. I have had people tell me, numerous times, that "Deity X gave me a message for you." So far, every time I cross-checked it with a priest or priestess or god-servant of Deity X, the message came back, "No, my patron/matron has no message for you."

Second, are you sure about the message? It's not unusual for us to misinterpret a divine directive, especially if we have our own fears about the matter. Divination may clarify the situation. Perhaps you are meant to do something, but not tomorrow, and not this year. Perhaps a symbolic approximation of that ritual will suffice. It's also possible that the entire issue is your own, and you superimposed it upon a simple goodwill touch (or disappointed touch) from a God/dess. Check, wait, and perhaps check some more before leaping off of a cliff. Gods are not stupid. They understand that we cannot always hear them clearly—in fact, perhaps it's unusual for most of us to *ever* hear them clearly—and if the deity knows you well enough to be asking things of you, they know you well enough to know what forms of message you will be more likely to take seriously. Another option is to ask them to repeat the message three more times, clearly and obviously, through some omen—a friend saying it out of nowhere, a truck driving by with the message on its side, that sort of thing. Don't go out of your way to look for and interpret omens—let them do their work. They are Gods, and they can do it.

Third, are you sure that it is in your long-term best interest, or that of the world? Those are two separate conditions, and admittedly they do often clash. An action may be good for you in the long run where you can't see it with your short mortal perspective, or it may be wholly inconvenient or even painful for you, but the world needs it and you are the best-placed person to do it (or perhaps at least the best-placed person that this deity can reach with the message). We all spend our lives deciding, from day to day, whether to make small-to-large sacrifices for the good of others. This is honorable work, and while it may not seem like it does you any good at all, I assure you that it does. On a soul-level it gives you credit, whether you call this *karma* or *wyrd* or *maegen* or anything similar. Nearly all spiritual traditions around the world validate the concept of positive soul-credit for good deeds, and I've never made such a sacrifice where I didn't learn *something* useful from it. This, too, can be checked with divination: ask whether it will be good for you in the long run, and whether it is a good deed that must be done because the world needs it. Then, although it may be cold comfort, you can feel proud that your deity trusted you with the task.

The nature of the deity in question also affects, by definition, the nature of your response. Some God/desses enjoy it when you argue with them, even if you never get your own way, because it's part of how they train you to question situations and think more deeply about them, or because they have argumentative natures and enjoy the process. (Trickster Gods and war Gods often fall into this category.) Others want their worshipers to obey orders and trust in the wisdom of the outcome. (Gods of Death or Justice and strongly elemental deities often seem to be very fond of this.) Some are willing to take a very hands-on approach and give you plenty of guidance (assuming that you are clear enough to hear it), and some feel that you would be better off figuring it out on your own (hunter deities and love goddesses are famous for this attitude). Some are fine with watching you reject their advice and fall on your face, so long as you learn something from it; others take it as a point of offense if you ask for help and then turn it down. So whether you argue or negotiate, and how the argument would best be framed, should be considered in the light of all the above factors.

If you take the advice of a spirit and it goes wrong, one of three things happened: First, they might have been wrong. It's possible. How possible depends on the nature of the spirit, whether the situation is their specialty, and what aspect of that spirit you were asking. (However, it's much more likely for us to get it wrong than for them to do so.) Second, you might have misinterpreted their instructions, in which case it's on you, and I strongly advise you to look thoroughly at this possibility and perhaps get some divination on the subject before you leap to the assumption that the Gods themselves have screwed up. Third, it's possible they chose for the long-term good and not the short-term convenience, and the result is a necessary disaster from which something positive can grow. Again, divination can help sort this out; I also recommend calling on Gods who have links to Fate and Destiny, as they may have a longer view of the situation. (Remember that more than one of these possibilities can be in play in any given situation.)

### Human Influences

Another intriguing question is that of our ability to influence the Gods. While I do not believe that we created the Gods, nor that we can kill them by ignoring them (or most ancient western deities would no longer be around to worship), it cannot be denied that we have some kind of influence on them, just as they affect us. If nothing else we can honestly say that we have an effect on their connection to this world. If we ignore them, they may not cease to exist, but their "phone line" to our world does seem to go down after a time. They still carry on with their own lives, but we are not a part of their sphere. They may be saddened by this, but their core being does not center around our needs.

Another way in which we affect Gods over time is by pressuring them to change in order to suit our needs. A colleague of mine (Linda Demissy of Montreal, priestess of Lokabrenna Kindred) pointed out that Gods often take on attributes and specialties over the centuries as humans beg for it; she used the Japanese deity Inari as an example. In Shinto, Inari began as a deity of rice agriculture and *kitsune* (shapeshifting spirit-foxes), and was depicted sometimes as an old man, sometimes as a young woman, and sometimes as an androgynous bodhisattva. Inari's specialty was agricultural prosperity, but then coastal people began to honor him for prosperous fishing as well. Soon other industries such as blacksmithing and warfare were added to his portfolio, and since Inari's shrines tended to get set up near the "pleasure quarter" of cities, she became a patroness of actors and whores. Modernly, she is prayed to for any aspect of prosperity, industry and finance; a number of Japanese corporations (including a major cosmetics company) have a shrine to Inari at their corporate headquarters and consider him their patron. Nearly a third of Shinto shrines honor Inari, a deity who is not even accounted for in any Shinto text, and has no history written about most of her "newer" talents.

One could speculate that if enough people pray to a small-time rice deity, sending energy for a wider range of purposes, that deity will eventually expand their sphere of influence to those purposes. At the very least, it would be a matter of trial and error on our part; certainly centuries of human beings experimented with praying to Gods A, B, and C for Cause X and noted what got results. The ancients were nothing if not practical, because they had to be.

Gods can also change their behavioral characteristics over time in order to fit in with changing human mores. One example of this is the differences in cultural behavior between the *orisha* of African tribes, who have either been influenced by Islam or are still practicing the unadulterated rites of their tradition, and the *orisha* of various African-diaspora religions, which had to adapt to Catholic values, sometimes taking on saint-names, in order to survive. Even if they are the same beings, they have had to adjust to very different cultural rules for their trans-continental worshipers. The African form of an *orisha* may uphold the rules of one culture's ideas about their specialty just as firmly as their African-diaspora aspect will uphold the very different rules of their adopted culture. (This is another example of how Gods are really more about values than rules, a concept which we will delve into in another chapter.)

## Searching For Gods

So how do we find out about any particular God or Goddess—what they like, what they don't like, what sort of people they might have an affinity for, what their gifts are, how they like to be dealt with? In some cases we have a great deal of (perhaps conflicting) material; for others, we have huge gaps in the information, or perhaps only a name and nothing more. One can deal with this problem in many ways, including the popular method of deciding that there is no way to recover that information, so if there isn't enough to work with regarding a particular spirit, one shouldn't even bother. This is an approach that seems to ignore the assumption that the Gods and spirits still actually exist, and if anyone has that information, they do—and who knows what spoor they have left in various places? Therefore, it's a matter of searching for clues, not only about the nature of a God but about ways to properly acquire their phone number, as it were, and ask them straight out.

It's possible to conceive of the search for the nature of a particular deity in the same way that one would think of hunting a large and somewhat dangerous animal whose existence is still in doubt. Many people claim to have seen the creature, but its habits are still uncertain. Different people have stories about the creature, some of them remarkably similar even though those people can be proven to have been unaware of each other. On the other hand, some tales are strikingly different. There are old stories written down about its existence from scholars who took down tales told by various wide-eyed, apprehensive peasants; but these, too, conflict with each other. By comparing all the accounts—historic and modern, regardless of differences, one can carefully construct a picture. If new information is brought in, it is compared to the existing stories to see if it can fill in missing pieces. If it doesn't match, it is not repudiated but carefully put aside; sometimes later evidence will be brought in which makes sense of the apparent anomalies.

This is the naturalist's method, and there are those who will bridle at the idea of me suggesting it, because *that's a method that sounds vaguely scientific, and science and faith are indelibly at odds, aren't they?* I would counter that when science is done right, it is done with a sense of wonder at the immense and amazing synchronicity of all Creation and how it develops, and the hunt for new discoveries becomes not plundering but gratitude for each gift of unfolded knowledge. I would also say that this ought to be the true spiritual sense of "naturalist"—one for whom the observation and discovery of Nature is a sacred act. We, and the shrimp and the plankton and the jewelweed and lichen and the bear, are all part of that synchronous whole—and so are the Gods. One of the wonderful things about polytheism is that even when our Gods make their home in alternate dimensions and only stroll over to visit, they (and their Otherworlds) are not set apart from the same Creation as ours, to look down on it from a cut-off, separated place. They are integrally part of it as well, and that's why we can touch them in small ways through that great Web.

Of course, the obvious difference between tracking an animal and tracking a deity is that the process of tracking the latter may actually get their attention. This is not a bad thing, although it can be disconcerting to someone who does not expect it (and we'll discuss this possibility later). It's even more of a reason, however, to approach the process with a properly reverential attitude. For those who are flinching at the word "reverential", imagining that it means some sort of groveling and thinking one's self unworthy, I would interpret the term instead as the classic "sunset moment"—you know, when you see the particularly dazzling sunset and your reaction is an overpowering "Wow!", often accompanied by a vague feeling of happiness, of how cool it is to be in a world where such things occur. That's what I think of when I strive to make my process of discovering the Gods more reverential, and I've never met a deity who disliked that particular attitude. (Of course, if there are any, perhaps they are so offended that they don't talk to me anyway, so I wouldn't know.)

This is the true nature of sacred scholarship: it is reverential, it remembers at all times that it is describing observations about People who are both humanlike and beyond human, and most importantly it takes all sources of information into account. It's not just the study of dusty old books; actual human experience must be part of the process. No good naturalist would restrict themselves to hundred-year-old accounts of sightings for a creature who still exists in its natural habitat, surrounded by people who live closer to that creature and might see it amble by their chicken house. If you really want to know, you have to get into the field.

So, drawing out the metaphor, what does "the field" consist of when we're discussing Gods? You can start with going to their archetypal stomping grounds. This doesn't necessarily refer to their human country of origin, although if you're dealing with a deity who is also the "spirit" of a particular area, that may eventually become necessary. What I'm referring to is the place where their energy is reflected. If this is an ocean goddess, get yourself to the seaside. If it is a deity of learning, go to a library or university. Study what that deity values, and in correlation, what sort of people dedicate themselves to that subject. What kind of personality traits do the best ones have? It's not so much that the deity will automatically have those traits as that the deity will value people with those traits, which can tell you something about who they might choose as a priest or other "special" follower. It may also be valuable information for someone who wants to approach that deity for some long-term purpose—might it be useful to develop those traits in themselves, as a kind of pre-offering, out of courtesy? Similarly, learning something significant about their preferred subject areas is a similar courtesy. It's like bothering to find out that Joe likes beer as a hospitality gift, is allergic to dogs, and wants you to take your shoes off in his house; knowing these small things will make Joe that much more well-disposed toward you when you go to visit.

It's also important to take into account all the subjects (and people, and other Gods/spirits) that this deity *doesn't* like. We are, in many ways, shaped as much by what we avoid and abjure as what we desire and value. This goes for Gods and spirits as well. Knowing that some agricultural deities prefer their food-gifts minus chemicals and agribusiness production, or that some sea gods like their fish offerings from small family fisherboats rather than industrial lines, or that deities X and Y should never be invoked in the same breath or have altars placed next to each other can save you from inadvertently offensive offerings. However, it also gives you insight into their character, and what sort of people they find uncomfortable. Try not to evidence too many of those personality traits if at all possible during dealings with them. As an example, a war god will probably be more favorably disposed to someone courageous and direct than someone fearful and indecisive. A mother goddess will probably be more interested in someone loving or protective or compassionate than someone cold and intellectual. There are always exceptions, of course—and more often than not those exceptions indicate that the deity in question has taken someone on as a project, helping them to achieve the qualities that they lack.

The next part of being in the field is talking to people who have a strong relationship with that deity. Here it's crucial to keep in mind that Gods approach different people in different ways, and ask widely varying things of them. Keep an open mind, even when—perhaps *especially* when—their experiences differ from yours. How many times have you met a friend of a friend, talked about your mutual friend, and discovered that they knew a side of them that you never got to see? It can sometimes be the same for Gods and spirits. Of course, it's also possible that they are having a dramatic relationship with a sock puppet in their head, but for the moment, neutrally set aside what they have said and don't call your jury back in until there is more information.

Another good reason for talking to living people is that the Gods are not static. Or, rather, part of them is static, and part of them is not. They don't live in linear time, remember? That means that you can actually interact with older and younger forms of a deity—both older and younger in the sense of their time in this world, and older and younger in the sense of the story of their life. The latter axis means that you can actually interact with forms of them as they were once, further back in their myth, which is a fascinating experience. Also fascinating is the idea that due to nonlinear time, the fact that some part of them is still living that past moment (for good or ill) is much more true than it is with humans who can only be that past person in vague memory. The former axis means that they keep changing and matching pace with the modern world—granted, some faster or more enthusiastic than others, but they do still change and adapt. Their relationships with modern devotees are the windows through which they do it, so talking to these people might get you a better sense of how the modern God/dess has changed and acclimatized.

What you're doing is the sacred art of piecing together the nature of a deity. Don't think that their nature is unknowable—it isn't, although their long-term plans may be. We may not be able to comprehend everything about a given deity, but isn't that true for human beings as well? No matter how well you think you know them, they may suddenly surprise you ... but you can know them well enough to figure out what to get them for a birthday present, when they can be trusted to show up, and what about them is glorious and worthy of your friendship and love.

## Pantheon Protocols

Few of us were raised in a polytheistic worldview, and so it can take us a while to get used to the idea. Our minds still drift toward assuming that there is a one true way, somewhere; a rulebook full of detailed assumptions that are true for every God and spirit out there ... and there aren't, except in a very general way. How do human beings want to be treated? We can make generalities, but if we grabbed ten people from radically different places and times, we'd have trouble doing more than that. Culture, past experience, and personalities are just too diverse. That's true for Gods and spirits, too.

Now I have to make a small detour into the matter of human culture and Gods, and how they affect each other. While the indigenous spirits of earth and fire and water, etc., have been with us since the beginning of life on this Earth, the Gods with their own cosmologies and Otherworlds seem to have made contact with us somewhere in the Paleolithic era. There is a point in the archaeology where we see the appearance of shamans, "specialized" human beings with the neurological ability to connect and communicate with noncorporeal entities. We don't know exactly what happened, but in spirit-aided glimpses of our collective ancestry I've seen the vague panorama of a possible past. Someone with just that extra edge of psychic talent connects with the natural spirits of this world, and they help to breed more of that talent into the line. (We'll discuss how that works at a later point in the book.) Their descendants forge relationships with the spirits in order to help their people to survive better, and somewhere along the line someone gets good enough to break the barrier not just between the perceptible world and the non-perceptible world in this place, but into another place ... and attracts attention.

This begins the long and complicated relationship of humanity and deities. I won't go into how those connections were forged and made stronger—perhaps only our ancestors can tell that tale—but it follows the cosmic principle of Like Attracts Like. Prehistoric humans were not identical, and neither were their tribes. Each small group of human beings was different, shaped by its geography and climate, genetics, sustenance, local flora and fauna, and the legacy of its strongest and best ancestors. This evolving uniqueness of culture called to a specific group of entities on the other side of the Veil, who made contact based on affinity. We did not create them, nor they us, and the fact that Norse

Gods live in a cold, snowy place while Maori Gods live in a rocky desert is not because we mentally placed them there, but because the universal forces that shaped us, shaped them as well in similar ways, and drew like to like.

Of course, the question remains: How much did we affect each other? It's certain that we allied first with local spirits and then with alien Gods out of survival. It was an evolutionary advantage to have access to forces who had knowledge and power that we didn't. It's quite likely that they affected our cultures with their own, although there is no way to know how, exactly. Did we—and do we—affect them? It's even harder to nail down proof for that, but modern dealings with deities do seem to reveal that they understand, at least, our current time and customs, even if they have grown far apart from their own. It might be speculated that our move away from the Gods allowed our culture to change radically from ones that had an affinity to, and had been partly shaped by, their own.

More specifically, this means that each ancient and/or indigenous culture is working with a different set of Gods and spirits, and their methods of spirit-handling will be similarly culture-specific. As an example of how this makes things frustrating for non-polytheists, we can look at the aggravation of anthropologists (and some modern spiritual practitioners) when they try to find one single set of tools and protocols for shamans and spirit-workers all over the world. Why do spirit-workers from one culture develop certain practices and not others, when a spirit-worker on the other side of the world works with all the practices that the first one ignores?

The answer is that the protocols for dealing with noncorporeal entities will be determined by the preferences of the particular entities that the shaman or spirit-worker has been dealing with for thousands of years. As those preferences will differ—sometimes drastically—from those of another pantheon, so will the protocols and methods that their human interface will adopt. One pantheon of spirits may be fine with "their" human beings railing at them and perhaps even threatening them to help; that may not work out well at all with another pantheon. Some are high-courtesy; some are more rough and direct. Some are gentler and some are more brutal, as a group. In fact, it's really impossible to understand why shamanic practices are so different the world over unless you fully accept how different spirits are from each other ... which requires fully understanding polytheism. This is why the practice of a Maori *matakite* will be different from mine, and we're both different from a Korean *mudang* or an Inuit *angakok* or a Siberian shaman—because we're working with different entities.

Some cultures still have detailed rules about what it is appropriate to offer any specific deity or spirit in their cosmology, not to mention how it is appropriate to show them, or how they manifest their personalities. Many others, however, have lost this information. Those of us with spiritually impoverished traditions need to do what we can to recover that knowledge, as well as making modern connections that may do just as well to fill in the gaps.

In most (I don't dare say *all*) pantheon protocols, however, there is an expectation of what a friend of mine calls the FEE principle—fair energy exchange. You don't get something for nothing, except in rare cases when Someone decides to help you out on a whim because they like you—and even then, they probably have an agenda that you don't see. In my own shamanic tradition, when one wants a favor, one makes an offering to the God or spirit first, not as payment but as a love-gift. It's a way of saying: "I want us to be in relationship of some kind, if only for this one transaction. I care about you as a being, and I ask that you care about me." No matter what happens after that, the gift is theirs—you don't take it back if it turns out that they cannot give you what you want.

Then you wait to see if your wish can be granted. If you are worried, you may want to get some divination to check on whether they are willing or able to grant it. If the results are positive, you wait. If you get what you ask for, that's when you give the thank-you gift. Every interaction you initiate should have both the before-gift and the after-gift involved, so plan accordingly.

Why bother with offerings at all? After all, the god in question can't actually eat the physical food or smell the physical incense or use the physical money (unless they are currently possessing a human body). This situation puts us in mind of a tale about a Pacific Islander culture that was being converted to Christianity by missionaries. The missionaries watched the Polynesian priests lay out food offerings for the gods and spirits, and then, later that night, after the ritual was over, the food was passed out to the people to eat. "Aha!" cried the missionaries. "See, the gods didn't really eat the food; you did. Your gods can't be real."

The Polynesian priests looked at the missionaries as if they were crazy, or at least a little ignorant. "The gods eat the spirit part of the food, and we eat the body of the food," they said. "Didn't your religion teach you that?"

So how do we create "spirit food", or the spiritual aspect of any offering? First, the principle of animism states that anything natural already has an indwelling spirit. For man-made items, one should bless them, or charge them with your own energy, which gives them a spirit form. Just holding them and stroking them can put in enough of your own energy to make them an appropriate offering. Deities from some cultures prefer that you leave the item for them indefinitely, out of respect; others are fine with you taking back the physical part of the offering, especially if it is perishable food and should be eaten. In most cases, the food will be blessed, and is edible; the spirits may have taken the life force, but they put something back in return. However, in some cases that doesn't happen, and eating food offerings will be eating dead, drained food. It will still have nourishment, but nothing in the way of life force. In general, one can tell intuitively if the spirits have blessed the food and want you to eat it, or have claimed it for themselves. Just reach out your hand toward it, as if your hand was a divining rod, and you can usually feel either a sense of welcome or a sense of repelling. If you feel your hand being strangely repelled, leave it and dispose of it in fire or earth later on.

To create an offering, you can draw from a number of different qualities associated with any particular deity. In the last chapter we discussed how to look for these qualities; in this one, we'll go into how to put the information together.

> ❖ **Colors:** Some Gods have specific colors that are associated with them. These are often drawn from their natural-world associations; for example, Thor is usually associated with sky blue while Gaea may be represented by any number of earth tones, but is partial to green. In other cases, the original source of the color choice may be entirely lost to us—perhaps in the connotations of that color in an ancient society, or even in an Otherworld. When deciding to decorate an altar, make a ritual garment, or give a colored offering when there is no specific color association in written sources, first check to see if this is a deity of a natural process or subject which has a color (sky, earth, river) and go with those shades. If they are instead a deity of an abstract subject (such as healing or war or learning), it is generally acceptable to use a color that you strongly associate with that subject. I may associate the healing goddess Eir with red due to her gift for surgery; my friend feels that green is more appropriate for her healing gift. She seems to take both

colors with no problem. Remember also that it's not uncommon for a deity to have more than one color.

❖ **Numbers:** This is rarer, but some Gods have numbers associated with them. The Afro-Caribbean *orisha* or *lwa*, for example, each have combinations of colors and numbers that can be made into devotional bead necklaces. Mercury has long been associated with the number three, while both Odin and Hela like the number 9, being at the top and bottom of a World Tree with nine worlds. If the deity you're looking at has no number associated with them in older sources, you may want to look into numerology and select a number that has similar associations—for example, six is traditionally associated with love and harmony, and would be a good fit for most love deities.

❖ **Items:** This is often the easiest part, if there is any mythos at all still existing. Some Gods have specific items associated with them—Zeus's thunderbolt, Apollo's chariot and lyre, Thor's hammer, Nuada's silver hand. Other items may appear in their stories and make sense to have as their symbols. However, if an item appears in their story in such a way that it does them harm, it is unlikely to make a good impression if you assign it as their symbol. (Don't put mistletoe on an altar to Baldur, or involve eagle symbolism when trying to contact Prometheus, for instance.)

❖ **Animals:** Many deities have animals associated with them as symbols, such as Aphrodite's dove or Poseidon's horse. Some have specific pets or service animals—steeds, guard dogs, messengers, etc. What this means, especially when it comes to symbolic animals, is that the deity in question has forged a good relationship with the overarching "grandparent" spirit of that animal—such as Grandmother Cat or Grandfather Boar. If you are having trouble getting a message through from the deity in question about their nature, it is possible to ritually ask the Grandparent spirit of their symbolic animal, if they have one, just as you'd ask someone about their friend—and with the same level of respect.

- **Plants:** As with animals, many Gods have special friends among the Greenwights, often distributed without apparent regard for the nature of the deity. Both beautiful Aphrodite and stern Holda love roses; both Odin and Hades love parsley. Also as with animals, it's good to keep in mind that these are not just random vegetable symbols that happen to be dedicated to these Gods. The Grandparent deva of that plant is a personal friend of that deity, you can be sure, and as such they can be a source of information. They can also be a broker, making an introduction between you and that God. Remember also that trees as well as small plants fall into this category, and that edible plants can be made into food offerings.

- **Stones and Metals:** By "stones", I don't necessarily mean precious and semiprecious gems like amethyst and amber, although those sorts of stones certainly do have a long and impressive history of being associated with various deities. However, plain old rocks from specific places dedicated to a deity, or places under their "jurisdiction", will do as well. Beach rocks for sea gods, desert rocks for desert gods, stones from the foot of the statue in the middle of the university for the deity of learning. For metals, there is of course the issue of the older metals (silver, gold, iron, etc.) and the newer ones that our ancestors would not have been able to extract (aluminum, niobium, etc.), which don't have specific associations. Still, as I've said before, the Gods change, and they might take a shine to new metals. Some trickster gods and inventor-types certainly have.

- **Food and Drink:** This is the most common form of offering, whether for spirits of the Dead, elemental spirits, or Gods. One possible option is to recreate the food of the culture closest to that deity. Another is modern food that has an affinity to them in some way—through color, shape, or "jurisdiction affinity", such as bread for harvest gods or fish for sea gods. If the deity is associated with a livestock animal, it is generally acceptable to offer them the meat, but if they are associated with a wild animal, an offering of the meat of that animal might be an appropriate offering or it might be highly offensive, depending on the deity. Keep in mind that while many Gods love alcohol, a few eschew it completely and will be offended if you offer it. You can also have a ritual "dinner with Gods" by serving them food along with you and giving them a place at your table.

- ❖ **Music:** If you can play music yourself, this is a wonderful offering, but even if you can't, it's a gift to carefully select music that reminds you of the deity (or your love for them, if you have that kind of relationship), and play it for them. Dancing to it, even if in private, while focusing on how wonderful they were, is also appropriate.

- ❖ **Service Offerings:** This is one of the highest offerings you can give. Doing an act of service that is an activity under the jurisdiction of that deity, for the sort of person they love, is a way of being their hands in the world. Whether it's babysitting for a tired young mother in the name of Demeter, giving shelter to a returning veteran in the name of Mars, cleaning up a natural area in the name of Gaea, or donating money to travelers' aid association for Mercury, giving service to the world not only honors them but furthers their work and their goals. While the Gods do not exist to help us and our world, they do care, and helping to make the world a better place in their name is a glorious thing.

## The Best You Can Give

One of the questions that has been strongly debated in my Pagan group, and probably will continue to be, is whether an offering or an act of service is acceptable if it is not given or done with the whole heart. As with so many things in polytheism, this too depends—on the deity and their relationship to you (trusted patrons will know you well and better understand your struggle), the difficulty of the circumstances, and whether it is done publicly as an example or in private circumstances. Obviously a gift given with the whole heart is always better, but if half-hearted service is the best you can manage at the moment, then do your best and the Gods will understand. What generally isn't acceptable is thoughtless throwaway gifting, done with no real intent at all. It's better to struggle with your emotions over the offering—which at least is energy put into it, and shows that you understand the seriousness of the gift—than to do something perfunctory or meaningless.

If you're not sure whether an offering is appropriate or will be accepted, the best way to tell is to build an altar to that deity. It can be very simple—a box or shelf with a cloth over it, a candle to light, some symbol you're fairly sure of. (It can, of course, be more elaborate as well.) The altar is the door you create for the energy of that deity to come through. Sit in front of it with your offering and clear your mind. Breathe deeply and focus on just looking at their altar, then reach out your hand with the possible offering in it and pay attention to what happens. Try hard not to expect or assume what you will feel; just empty your mind and reach out. If you feel a sense of pressure and your hand doesn't want to go all the way to the altar, it's a no. If your hand goes easily to the altar and deposits the item, it's a yes. If it seems pulled there like a magnet, it's a definite yes. Gods have their ways of making things known, even through all the distractions that bombard our souls.

If a deity who is not well-known, has few followers, and has not had much of a connection to this world for some time, asks you to do something that was once part of their worship but is now not possible (or, perhaps, not possible without someone going to prison), it is within your rights to explain that the world has changed, and this gift can no longer be given. Do not believe that a God cannot learn anything new. They can. They are People, even if they are less messy and more monolithic in their natures than we are. It is a gift to them to explain this, and then it is very much in your best interest to figure out a way to give a different form of that gift, one that is appropriate to this time and place, and that you can cleanly offer. Your gift should, ideally, be to the same end purpose as the original offerings. Be creative—you'd be surprised what you can come up with. (One friend of mine had his patron deity ask for the sacrifice of his right arm, and he immediately had it liberally tattooed with the symbols of that God, announcing, "There! My right arm is now your temple." His patron, according to him, seemed to be delighted.)

Make sure, however, that you understand the point of the original offerings, or you'll get it wrong. For example, some deities were given the gift of the sacrifice of a life, whether human or animal. This might have been about giving them a new servant, or a livestock animal of their own, which would have the same spiritual potency as giving them any other valuable household item. This was done by invoking the magic of mirroring: the idea that what is whole here is broken to pass through the veil and become whole there, and vice versa. Invoking this spiritual dimension has long been a way to get a physical offering through the veil separating us. However, the sacrifice might instead have been done to give the deity a gift of powerful energy, both the life-force of whatever died and the emotions of those who had to watch. If it was an animal, it might have been a way for that God/dess to give a gift of food to their beloved people through your sacrifice, the energy of which was also a gift to them. (And, of course, sometimes sacrifices were made to the Gods for purely human reasons, such as political power or conspicuous display, which happens in all religions.) Find out—through divination or through prayer to them—why those original sacrifices were given, and copy the purpose, not the form. Anything that is valuable to your everyday life, and which is a struggle to afford or let go of, can "go through the mirror" for them. Doing something that is hard for you—and, even better, getting a group of people to do a difficult thing together—can provide both energy and show your willingness to inconvenience yourself for your deity. Even the effort of finding something new to give them—which can then be copied by worshipers everywhere—is a gift in and of itself. Don't let the form of the offering distract you from the point of making it. For instance, while I cannot afford to build whole temples to Gods, I've built quite a few online shrines to them, and I was surprised how quickly some of the Gods showed their appreciation afterwards. (An online shrine also widens the scope of their worship to people who would never otherwise know them.)

As a more controversial example, some Pagan groups have used my land to make respectful livestock sacrifices to their Gods, because they want the chance to give a gift in the old-fashioned way. However, we aren't those peasants for whom a sheep was several meals we wouldn't otherwise have. That kind of financial sacrifice isn't real for us. Instead, when we do these (rare) rituals, I encourage everyone watching to actively deal with their issues around death, around the fact that we do not see where our food comes from but can thoughtlessly eat meat plastic-wrapped from the supermarket, and have been trained not to think about it in the very Pagan terms of all life feeding on life, and what that means, and how it is sacred. I encourage people to explore their ambivalence as they watch, to plumb the depths of their feelings, and to offer that struggle to the Gods. That is a sacrifice that we can honorably offer, and are the better for it. And afterwards, of course, the animal is cooked and offered to the community as a feast, a gift in that deity's name to their beloved people. Offerings are all about willingness and intent, and believe me when I say that will be challenging enough to give.

## The Search for Morality and Other Complications

Ancient Western cultures did not draw their rules of ethics and morality from their religion, or at least not from specific rules built into the faith and recited as part of its known canon. Generally, codes of morality were built into the culture; one followed the rules set by one's society, because one wished to live in it. Considering that in many of those ancient cultures, there wasn't really much of a choice—leaving one's homogenously-cultured homeland was difficult and meant a lifetime of exile—those codes were usually accepted like the air one breathed or the water one drank—sometimes difficult, but no more so than the difficult parts of the rest of existence. An ancient Roman soldier, for example, would take a particular moral action not because that was what a good follower of Mars would do, but because it was what a good Roman would do. Priests, mystics, and other professionally religious people might have deity-specific rules, but most of those rules were more likely to be about specific ritual actions that their patron deity might find pleasant or worshipful, rather than codes of morality.

The Gods, on the other hand, might uphold those moral codes—not by their function but by their actions—or they might show how they, as Gods, might be above that morality. At first glance, one would assume that the Gods and the religion seemed to be more affected by the culture than the culture was by the religion. This brings us back around to the difficult question of how much we, as humans, influence the Gods—or, perhaps, how much our tales of them are veiled through our own cultural filters and assumptions. Instead of walking down any of these roads, I would prefer instead to revisit the concept introduced in the last chapter—the idea that Gods, and Otherworlds, are drawn to people (and peoples) to whom they have an affinity, whether of geography or culture or both. This concept is less about chicken-and-egg arguments of who formed whom, and more about synchronicity, and the cosmic version of the Law of Attraction—*like attracts like*. While I do not rule out the idea that the Gods influence us, nor even that we have the power (however limited) to influence the Gods, our cultural interweaving begins with attraction, not blunt creation. Once we are synchronous with the worlds of our Gods, we can begin to affect each other, but not until then.

If we take this point as a given, it puts us as modern Western people into an odd situation. Most of us were not born into ancient polytheistic religions or even their modern versions, and are converts from other faiths which contain rules of morality as part of their doctrine. We grew up with those morals (and with the idea that one could fall back unquestioningly on religion for one's morals). We also live in a pluralistic society made up of many different cultures and their ethical codes, none of which are the ones our Western Pagan ancestors lived in and under. These varied cultures compete to get their codes integrated into the overarching social laws of the land, and between that competition and our increased levels of communication, cultural codes change exponentially quicker than they ever have in the past. Rather than simply being wistful about bygone eras, we need to cope realistically with the fact that we live here and now. Even strict Reconstructionists admit that we cannot really live fully in the mindset and culture of our ancestors all the time, or even completely comprehend what that would have been like. Besides, some moral codes do not translate well into modern culture; such concepts as blood-vengeance, nonconsenting slavery, and human sacrifice might have been perfectly acceptable and even mandatory for the ancients, but they aren't going to go over well today. Given all these facts, what does it mean for us that our group connection to the ancient Gods is based not on culture, but on faith?

From current observation, it seems that the Gods are able to adapt to us—enough, at least, to be willing to reach out and make bonds with us individually and as groups. If anything, they are reaching out at a rate unlike anything seen before this century, an interesting phenomenon that we will discuss later. However, the attention of individual deities—however wonderful and spiritually inspiring—still leaves us with the issue of morality. Polytheistic Gods often act in ways that we, commonly and modernly used to all Gods being paragons of unalloyed Goodness, are horrified by. Their rules may differ from one God to the next—what's right for a war God is not necessarily going to be embraced by a love Goddess, or a trickster God. Indeed, as one worshiper put it to me, no matter what your desired course of action, if you look hard enough you can find some deity in some pantheon who would approve of it. To worshipers who grew up with the Christian bible or the Judaic Torah, the art of building a moral code out of tales of questionably-moral exploits of deities and ancestors, usually by doggedly ignoring the overwhelmingly inappropriate and carefully selecting out the few pieces that shore up your list of existing rules, may seem heart-sinkingly familiar. It leaves us with the quandary that all religious moralists hate: the obligation to openly pick and choose, and the inevitability that there will be mass disagreement.

With our religious views in a state of revival and flux as we slowly discover our balance in this matter, most modern polytheists choose to create their own codes of morality from external sources. Since, as I've commented repeatedly here, many of the most immediate sources are that of the dominant monotheistic religious forms which have—rather successfully—imprinted themselves onto Western culture, it means that we cannot choose blindly from what the dominant culture, or our upbringing, offers us. We bear the burden of sorting through each choice and asking ourselves, not "Is this what God X would do or not do?" but "Is this likely to lead to the sort of world in which all my Gods would want to live?"

The truth is that where the influence of the Gods does affect our morality—and sometimes fairly drastically—is not in their personal codes of behavior, but in their values. For us, it is not so much that our Gods tell all their worshipers how to behave so much as they ask us to value what they value, and act accordingly. For example, one of the Gods that I love deeply is an agricultural deity, and in honor of him I have become invested in eating food that is grown in a more ecologically and spiritually correct way, and supporting organic farming. I serve a Death Goddess, and for her I give aid to the dying and the survivors, and I support green burial. I honor a number of earth deities, and ecology is important to me. I love and revere a God of the outcasts, and I speak and write for them. Each of these values, chosen mindfully, helps to shape my code of ethics. When we ask the Gods "What morals should we hold?" they do not answer with "You must *do* this," so much as "This *way of being* is important."

This reflects the fact that the Gods are in harmony with their Universe. That includes the Gods who are troublemakers, whose sacred job is pointing out flaws to battle complacency, or doing the necessary but unpleasant deeds to move a situation out of stagnation. Harmony does not equal stagnation, even though we mortals who so value our convenience would like to see it that way. In Nature, there are continual challenges—to life, to territory, to nourishment, to general future prospects—and their purpose is to strengthen life, not merely to unfairly harass it. A God/dess's concept of harmony is broad enough—and insightful enough—to include challenges and oppositions within it. They are aware that the Web of Life (and that includes not just life in this material Universe, but existence everywhere) depends on its own checks and balances to continually pull toward the middle of all oppositions, all binaries. Yet the two ends of any binary are sacred as well, even in their extremity, just as the middle points are as well. We are all born of parents, after all. The middle ground could not be sacred unless its pre-existing "progenitors" were as well, and sacred progenitors cannot do other than create a sacred union-point.

On a practical level, this brings us back once again to the fact that having multiple Gods can be as much of a strength as a weakness in developing a moral code. Polytheism gives us the chance to honor multiple sets of values—simultaneously, or in turn, as we choose—rather than simply giving us a list of moral actions and inactions. Ancient polytheistic pantheons usually included a wide variety of worthy sets of overlapping but not identical values, embodied by those Gods. In order for a sense of sacred balance to occur, that wide variety needed to exist. Modernly, it is expected that we will go about integrating these various sets of values into our lives in mindful ways that guide us in creating our own code of ethics. The whole nature of polytheism lends itself best to mindfulness rather than blindly following what is set in front of one to follow.

On the other hand, if this seems to leave the confused seeker in the lurch—and "Figure it out yourself!" is not a fair or useful answer to many people—this is where a good priest or minister or other spiritual leader can help. I should stress that the role of clergy in polytheistic religion is to aid someone in forming their own code of ethics, both by example and by teaching and discussing the various sets of values inherent in the nature of the Gods. This puts the clergyperson or spiritual leader in a more delicate place than a religion with a strict set of rules built into its doctrine, and requires more thought and finesse in helping any given seeker. Instead of simply saying, "This is what is right to do, and you must do it or some divine consequence will befall you," the polytheistic clergyperson needs to find a way to discern the interests and innate personality of the seeker and which deities he/she is attracted to (or who is attracted to him/her); to communicate the nature and values of the Gods of their pantheon (or pantheons, if it is an eclectic Pagan); to be honest about what is missing in the value set of any given deity and offer the viewpoint of a balancing one; and to walk the seeker through the process of creating their own ethical rules from this bouquet of divine value-sets without simply inserting a copy of their own world-view. This is a much more challenging ideal than simply laying down a list of rules which cannot be questioned if the seeker is to stay in the faith, and it is especially challenging when one considers that both the seeker and the priest may well both be battling baggage from a former worldview which requires that very approach.

Indeed, this concept of non-doctrinal morality may seem very unsatisfying to seekers who hope to be able to pick up a list of rules and run with it. Some Neo-Pagan groups—notably Reconstructionists or other groups who focus on one specific ancient religion—prefer to sidestep the issue of mindfulness and discernment by attempting to lift the values of the culture in which their religion was originally embedded. However, as I referenced above, the circumstances of the ancient world were different enough from our own that even this approach has yielded no less of a need to pick and choose, and no fewer arguments, than the system outlined above. Indeed, it may generate more arguments, if only because the goal of using ancient cultural values—having an integral set of rules which one need not question too deeply, and which fit into a specific ready-made worldview—tends automatically toward too much rigidity to survive the necessary discernment process without continual intra-group argument.

To be fair, it's not as if the ancients did not do several millennia's worth of work on the subject of ethics, and we need not reinvent the wheel when they made so many. If reading about the philosophies of the ancient culture of your Gods—or any ancient culture—inspires and influences you in creating your own code, then give thanks to the Ancestors and take the gifts they paid so dearly to pass down to us. If the work of picking and choosing comes easy to you, and seems obvious, then all the Gods bless you. The problems generally only come when people expect to be able to live wholly as people in a different and often conflicting era.

It's not an easy answer, but then when it comes to the Gods and the workings of the Universe, there is no such thing. I should also point out that the Gods love to see us struggle in this way—not because they are sadistic or enjoy our suffering so much, but because they take joy in seeing us grow, and conquer difficult obstacles, and come through it wiser people. They are also quite willing to reach out and give us aid in this struggle, if we are ready and open enough to accept it. Perhaps the best action that a clergyperson can take when it comes to helping a seeker down this path is to pray with them, often and sincerely, and ask that the Gods lay the answer before their eyes.

## Sacrifice, Smiting, and Silence: The Hard Parts Of Divine Relationship

One of the complaints—or, perhaps, warnings—that non-polytheists say about the ancient western Pagan gods is that they demand sacrifices, and they smite people when they are angry. When we use the word "smite" or "smiting", we are usually talking about the concept of a deity lashing out and punishing a human being because the human being has done something to offend the deity. If we look at the ancient myths, it's true that there are numerous accounts of the Gods doing both of these things. Usually their smites took the form of their greatest gifts—a sea god might send a tidal wave, and a love goddess might make someone fall in love with an inappropriate target.

For those of us who love and are drawn to the Gods, the question arises: are all instances of divine "punishment" designed to be a lesson for our growth, or are the Gods ever simply petty and wrathful and lashing out? As I discussed earlier, dealing with a deity's more humanlike aspects does raise the possibility of their behavior seeming more like petty human rage, but to how much of our suffering does this apply? Do Gods that we don't even know about smite us? Should we live in fear, all the time, like we often tend to assume our ancestors did?

The question of smiting also brings us to the question of Fear Of God. Abrahamic religions put a great deal of doctrinal energy into making sure that the followers of their God(s) were strongly motivated by fear of inappropriate behavior, which in turn was determined by the clergy of those faiths. Many modern monotheists grew up on Fear Of God, and for a good percentage of those who turn to Pagan faiths of all sorts, the hope is that this idea and motivation can be entirely left behind. Of course, one glance at any extant religious writings about our Pagan ancestors showed that they knew all about Fear Of God(s), so where does that leave us?

Before we go deeply into this issue, I need to make one statement that may seem like it goes against the spirit of my entire book so far. It seems clear that in ancient times, the wrath of the Gods—sometimes for no apparent reason—was part of how people explained natural disasters. In most cases when I discuss the practices of ancient peoples, you will not hear me dismissing them as ignorance. In fact, I believe that it is foolish to refuse to take their world view seriously ... but this is one area where I am making an exception and standing by it. Life back then was very hard, and disasters struck often—illness, accidents and weather alone could wipe out entire tribes of people. It is human nature to look for an explanation for such hardships, if only for some sense of control in being able to prevent them the next time around. Certainly it is possible that the spirit-workers of a tribe of people would make bargains with various spirits in order to bypass those troubles, and it is also possible that becoming lazy about the proper offerings and payment might induce some spirits to withdraw their blessings and perhaps even vent their wrath, but sometimes a storm was just a storm, and a plague just a plague. It may have made the folk feel better, however, if it was declared to be the wrath of a spirit who could then be appeased. Even if the spirit in question had nothing to do with the disaster, propitiating them might gain their aid in ceasing the blight.

However, that doesn't mean that Gods and spirits do not occasionally get out the cosmic clue-by-four. Do they do it only out of petty anger? Do they lash out in rage without thinking of the consequences, or is anything that could be considered a smite actually a carefully-placed lesson? That's a tough question, and as far as I can tell, it does vary to some extent depending on the deity or spirit that you are dealing with, their particular personality, and what aspect you are dealing with. However, when it comes to most Gods, it is best to remember the earlier point about them being parsimonious. They nearly always stack several purposes onto every action, and our own growth as beings—whether painful or pleasant—is almost always one of them. It's agreed by nearly all my fellow polytheistic Pagan theologians that if you assume that "smite" had no lesson contained in it for you, you're probably missing something. By their very nature as higher beings, Gods are led to help us evolve through their interactions with us. That doesn't mean that they'll necessarily do it in ways that we enjoy, but it does mean that we can assume there's probably a point to this—assuming, of course, that we are sure it's an actual "smite" and not just one of the many aforementioned random storms and plagues, physical and otherwise.

Traditionally, the best way to tell if something was bad luck, inevitable consequence, or divine wrath was to go to a priest/ess or diviner who specialized in such issues, and have them check on the situation. (As someone who fills that role for my community, I can definitely say that what plagues people is much more often the first two than the third option.) If that's not possible, another way to tell is the carefully-aimed and specific direction of the misfortune. If it teaches a direct and obvious lesson related to the specialty of that deity, or related to a known wrongdoing or offense toward that deity, then it's more likely to have their hand behind it.

The most common way for a deity or spirit to smite someone is simply to withdraw their blessings, and any good fortune accrued with those blessings. A classic example of this was a young woman who had sworn herself to Yemaya, the orisha of the ocean and motherhood, because she longed for children and a happy family. She married a man she loved and had three children, and all seemed to be well. However, her husband was a Muslim, and he disapproved of her keeping an altar to Yemaya as part of her sacred bargain. Eventually he bullied her into forswearing her goddess and getting rid of the altar, and in a matter of months they were homeless and their children had been removed by the authorities. What had been given could be taken away—and sometimes the main message is simply *Keep Your Word To Us*.

On the other hand, non-divine spirits do sometimes lash out at us with no thought but for their own pain and anger. The spirit of that pond over there isn't necessarily going to think about your future evolution when you throw trash into its home. It is protecting itself, and the lesson that you learn—assuming that you make the connection, which you may not—is to be more mindful of what you do and on whose life you are encroaching. The best way to handle the situation, if you just aren't sure and no information is forthcoming, is to ask yourself: "If there was a lesson in this, and it was to help me to be a better person and not just to make me suffer, what might that lesson be?" Sometimes when you follow that line of logic with an open mind and no resentment, the answers become much more clear.

Of course, what we perceive as a "smite" may simply be the Gods getting out a larger stick to make us pay attention, perhaps after more subtle messages were ignored. One of my "aha" moments in understanding why my Goddess often seemed harsh to me came when a friend was visiting for a week, and one of the goats on our farm gave birth to weak and premature triplets. The whole house mobilized to dry, warm, and feed them. When baby goats are born a little early, or get chilled at birth, they often decide that they are going on a hunger strike and refuse to eat. Twenty-four hours of this, of course, and they'll be dead, so we have to force-feed them with bottles and syringes when necessary. My friend sat watching while we wrestled with towel-wrapped infant kids on our lap, fighting us with everything they had in their weak little bodies, determined not to absorb their mothers' nourishing colostrum. Our running monologues to them were something along the lines of, "You stupid little creature! Will you please just drink the milk? It's good for you! I promise you that once you get the hang of this eating thing, you'll like it! Anyway, you'll die without it! I don't want to have to clean up your little corpse in the morning! What's wrong with you, damn it! Will you please just drink the damn milk?"

"I wonder," my friend said, "if the Gods sometimes feel exactly the same way about us."

Sacrifice is another point of difficulty for many people coming to polytheism in this era. Our ancestors made many sacrifices to the Gods—food, drink, tools that had been crushed or broken or thrown into bogs, and sometimes the lives of animals and even people. In each case, there was a difference between an offering and a sacrifice, in that a sacrifice was meant to be emotionally difficult to give over. That was the point—as a sacrifice prayer in the Pagan Book of Hours says:

> It is the nature of sacrifice
> To be difficult.
> If it was easy to throw away,
> It was no sacrifice.
> If you did not miss it
> It was no sacrifice.
> If it was not the best you could give
> It was no sacrifice.
> If it was not agonizing to choose,
> It was no sacrifice.
> If it did not make you waver at least once in your choice,
> It was no sacrifice.
> If it did not make you weep,
> It was no sacrifice.

This is possibly one of the most difficult parts for us to understand of the process of dealing with deities. First, we don't understand why the Gods would want us to suffer, especially if they care about us and do not wish us harm. Monotheistic religions have long fought the idealistic battle between the image of God as all-good and all-loving, and God as one who allows and perhaps even causes harm to come to human beings. Many of us bring the first (and more attractive) quality to or assumptions about our polytheistic Gods, declaring them entirely kind and loving toward us. This misses the point that the Good/Evil dichotomy is not part of our worldview. Things, people, and Gods aren't Good or Evil—they simple Are, and Are What They Are. To try to sort them into arbitrary categories based largely on their emotional appeal to our psyches—which are varied enough that we will never agree on anything sorted by those standards—is to misunderstand the nature of the polytheistic Universe. Pain is not always Evil. Sometimes it is the way that we learn to break down a wall and find a way out of our self-limiting personal labyrinths.

One of the flaws endemic to humanity is our tendency to take necessary and sacred things for granted. Sacrifice is one of the methods used by the Holy Powers to force us out of that pattern, if only for the category of sacrifice we are making. As I mentioned in the chapter on offerings, animal sacrifice was once the white-knuckled stress of knowing that you were giving a large chunk of your survival protein to the community in order to honor a deity, regardless of whether that would mean that your family went hungry for a short time in the future. Today it can be used to face the sorrow of how far removed we have made ourselves from the reality of the natural cycle, and what poisonous ambivalence, squeamishness, and denial-based illusions of neverending physical life it has implanted in us, and how much work we have to do in order to be in harmony with the natural world. Both of these sacrifices are honorable, because they make us more mindful of What Is, rather than pushing us toward What We Would Like To Be True. Similarly, sacrificing all your cigarettes to the sacred fire is an acknowledgement that you are willing to suffer in order to be more whole, and that you are willing to turn your guidance in this matter over to the Holy Powers who are being gifted. That mindfulness process can rarely be done without at least some pain, because we are flawed human beings. However, rather than castigating ourselves, we can face sacrifice with acceptance of the process, determination to see it through, and compassion for ourselves and each other.

It's never easy for any of us to dwell on these things for long, and that's a good reason for doing it in a supportive community ritual where we can see each others' striving, and support each other. While personal sacrifice done alone and isolated can be noble, it can also force us into accidental oubliettes—denial, despair, or arrogant obsession. Sacrificing together can be done with more humility, if the community ethic is one of compassion and honesty. However, alone or together, the moment of sacrifice can be the moment when the energy of the Gods break through for a moment, just long enough to ride the energy that we are putting out, to appreciate our efforts, and to touch us in blessing.

This brings us to one of the most painful issues of all when it comes to dealing with deities: what happens when you can't communicate with them well enough to know what they want of you? The truth is that most people will not be able to hear Gods and spirits all the time, and some may not ever hear them. We don't know why some people seem to be born with the "god-phone" and others aren't. We do know that it has nothing to do with whether they are ethical, or honorable, or sane, or even nice people. Regular two-way communication with Gods and spirits is never, as far as we can tell, based on merit. Plenty of people have this experience who aren't the most evolved characters around, and plenty of very good people do not get it. (The medieval mystic Julian of Norwich apologetically wrote that people must not think that her communications with saints made her a better person; that she knew many who were far better Christians than she, and she had no idea why the saints did not speak to them as well.) Some evidence points to the gift running in families; sometimes it seems completely random. Extreme physical experiences, such as coming very close to death, can apparently give some people the sudden ability to communicate with the Divine even when they've never been able to do it before.

Attitudes toward whether the average worshiper ought to be able to hear the Divine vary depending on cultural backgrounds. In parts of Neo-Paganism, for example, there is an assumption that the only reason that every human being doesn't walk around in constant conversation with Gods is because we were taught as children that it couldn't be true, and so we crippled that part of our minds. The corollary to this theory is that if we all just managed to really believe it could be done, it would happen—which general experience does not, unfortunately, bear out. Since we also have no doctrinal limits on who ought to be talking to the Holy Powers, this attitude blithely assumes that we could all be mystics and mediums if we only tried. This is in defiance of the fact that in tribal societies where everyone believes in Gods and spirits, the ability to see, hear, sense, and/or communicate with them is still not distributed equally. If that had been true in less "civilized" times, there would have been no need for the position of tribal shaman.

In contrast, Asian culture assumes that except for a few unusually gifted people, we are all born blocked to the presence of Spirit, and must strive to gain signal clarity over the course of our lifetimes. This is generally achieved with hard work—meditation, special diets, and other austerities. If one is diligent, one may eventually become clear enough to connect with the Divine, but it rarely comes as a free gift. Yet another view is that of some tribal cultures, which see the only way to achieve really good two-way communication with Spirit (or spirits) as being the deliberate practice of altered states. Theoretically, in this worldview, anyone can achieve an altered state using one of many techniques, but most people shouldn't do it because without the aid of the spirits themselves, it can all go terribly wrong. Since the only way to guarantee the aid of the spirits is to have enough natural talent to contact them, ask for their alliance, and be certain that the deal was successful, this sets the practice aside for those who are born with at least a small bit of the gift.

In monotheistic faiths, dogma often determines expectations. For some of those faiths, speaking to God is reserved for clergy, or in some situations special mystics who have been validated by doctrinal systems, either while they live or after they are safely dead and their various words can be reinterpreted. In others, congregants are encouraged to have a personal relationship with Deity, and the expectation is that if you believe thoroughly enough, and pray hard enough, you will be gifted with God's attention and presence. The god-phone, in these cultures, is used as a goad for further devotion, for as long as it works. In still other monotheistic denominations—especially ones who are suspiciously in reaction to the last sort of sect—it is emphasized that God does not talk to us (any more, or perhaps never did), but that we are watched anyway and must have faith in that fact. Here, mystic connection is seen as dishonesty or insanity, and faith in the absence of all evidence is seen as the most honorable road.

So how do we explain the difference between a mystic's experience and the "radio silence" endured by most people, most of the time? Is the idea of conversing with the Gods just setting people up for failure, and thus disillusionment? In my experience and that of most of the polytheists I know and love, there can be many reasons for "radio silence". One list of them was compiled by Kenaz Filan and myself when we co-wrote the book *Talking To The Spirits*, published by Inner Traditions Press, which was written at the same time as this book. It deals much more specifically with the problem of signal clarity and how to improve it, but any such work must come to terms with the fact that not everyone is going to find it easy, or even possible. Anyhow, here is our quoted list of potential obstacles:

> ❖ *You could do it if you tried, but you're not trying hard enough.* Most people didn't grow up with families who encouraged them to be aware of or

cultivate their subtler senses, and in fact most grew up in families who openly ridiculed such things. Children who had spirit-encounters were told that they were imagining things, and later they learned the association of "imaginary friends" with mental illness. This meant that many people have repressed what subtle senses they have, deeply enough that it may take decades to dig them back up again. Most people are also not encouraged to still their minds and listen, and our hurried lives often discourage this as well.

- ❖ *You're afraid of what might happen if the Gods spoke to you.* Divine contact could mean that you're crazy, according to much of the rest of society. It could also mean that the Gods were real and could never again be easily ignored or put aside when their existence in your life becomes inconvenient. In addition, people who were raised with the idea that prayer was primarily a form of confessing your faults to God may not want to know what God/the Gods/the spirits have to say, because they are afraid it will only be a litany of everything that is wrong with them. If you fear the voice of Spirit, even if only subconsciously, you will block it out.

- ❖ *Your psyche (or body, or both) is damaged to the point where your subtle senses have been blocked by the damage.* There are many factors that could contribute to this, including neurochemical illness, PTSD, chronic physical pain, drug use, alcoholism, or general ill health. As diviners, we have seen plenty of people with wrecked lives who come in asking, "What's my spiritual path?" and the answer that we receive from the Spirits is, "We're not even going to go there right now. You need to focus on the practical aspects of your life, and get off drugs, or take care of your health, or get out of your toxic life situation, or whatever it is that's wrecking your life and could be changed. Fix that first, no matter how long it takes, and then we'll talk about spiritual paths."

- ❖ *Your natural inborn neurological and energetic "wiring" is not able to sense things in this way.* This is a controversial reason; some spiritual thinkers believe that it is possible, and others don't. The idea that spirit-communication is dependent largely on the luck of neurology is a difficult one for many people to swallow, and of course there's no scientific proof either way. It does seem that the more impressive (and difficult to manage) psychic gifts run in families and can be genetically inherited, a fact which is used by proponents of the idea of neurological "spirit-wiring" to support their thesis. According to this view, being able to communicate with Spirit is an inborn gift held by only a few, and this is how it has always been. Just as not everyone can have perfect pitch or be an Olympic athlete or an Einstein-level physicist, not everyone can have the gift of the spirit-phone. On the other hand, some modern spiritual teachers feel that everyone has the potential for this gift, and inability is not an inborn lack but a problem of lack of practice, as in reason #1. There's also the issue of improving what you have; many religious traditions have practices of meditation and altered states that are designed to enhance and change the inborn "wiring". How effective this can be, and how far one can go with neurology that resembles a psychic brick, has been a matter of debate for centuries. (Raven's Note: Please check out the rest of *Talking To The Spirits* for that information, since it is beyond the scope of this text.)

❖ *It's your life's destiny this time around to concentrate on the physical world, at least for now.* There's no shame in living in the physical world and seeing its myriad beauty as sacred and worthy. People all have different life lessons to learn, and if yours is to appreciate this world rather than concentrate on Otherworlds, there's probably a very good reason for that. After all, someone has to do it! It is by no means a "lesser" destiny, and don't let anyone else tell you otherwise.

❖ *It's your life's destiny this time around to make your own decisions, without help or advice or influence from Spirit.* Again, everyone's life lessons are different. For some, the big lesson is trusting in the will of the Gods. For others, it is learning to trust themselves. This can be a temporary thing—*you need to figure this out yourself, it won't mean as much if you get a message from Beyond*—or it can be a life pattern. Ironically, we've found that while the people who have free rein on their life path complain about how much they crave some kind of direction, many of the spirit-ridden people on the other end of the spectrum whose lives are largely governed by divine will complain about how much they'd like to be able to do whatever they want with no direct spiritual consequences. The grass is always greener on the other side, which is a good indication that everyone involved is getting the experience that they need to evolve and grow, if not the experience that they might prefer.

❖ *It's your life's destiny this time around to learn to keep faith in the face of divine silence, and to model that faith to others who find themselves facing an unresponsive Universe.* This is perhaps the hardest reason of all, and the one that requires the most compassion from spiritual leaders if the individual is to fulfill their purpose. One of the most significant modern examples of faith in the face of divine silence was the Catholic nun Mother Teresa, who said bluntly that the single hardest part of her vocation was "...God's silence." She apparently received some sort of visitation earlier in her life which pushed her into helping the poor and dying in Calcutta, but after that she received nothing more for the rest of her days. Her constant round of self-doubt was evident in her writings and from her words to those who knew her, but so was her constant re-orienting once again to her faith. In *First Things*, Carole Zaleski writes of how Mother Teresa converted "her feelings of abandonment by God into an act of abandonment to God." Focusing on the idea of Christ's loneliness and sacrifice on the cross helped her to see her own silent isolation and sacrifice as embodying that moment as an everyday discipline. To say that some people may be fated, during this lifetime at least, to follow in Mother Teresa's path will not make us many friends, nor be satisfying to those who are shouting into the void to no avail. Mother Teresa herself clearly did not want that path, even though she made the absolute best of it, and most of us are not nearly as dedicated as she was.

The upshot of both the pressure in Neo-Paganism to be able to achieve mystical experiences out of nowhere, and the dismissal of any other road as spiritually useful and rewarding, sometimes results in the opposite extreme—people and groups who have come to firmly believe that the Gods aren't talking to anyone any more, and anyone who thinks otherwise is deluded or insane. When they come up with statements like "If you talk to the Gods, you're praying; if the Gods talk back, you're crazy," what they are doing is salving their justifiable pain in the face of unfair circumstances. (Although a friend of mine likes to retort, in these cases, "No, if they talk back, you're blessed.") It's hard to sit alone with your silence and the sock puppets in your head, and watch other people happily claiming to be in constant communication with their Gods. Perhaps they are, and perhaps they aren't. Someone who was a legitimate mystic or spirit-worker might be able to tell, but how can one trust what any of them might say, either? Besides, why do they get the god-phone, and not me? It's not like they're any better than me, after all.

It's easy to see how cynicism can cause a lashing-out reaction, but the best response to this attitude is not defensiveness but compassion. Of all the reasons we have uncovered for a lack of communication with the world of Spirit, the one reason that we have never encountered is that the individual is a contemptible human being, unworthy of spiritual attention. That has never happened in our experience, and as far as we can tell, that's not the way the Gods work. For those of you who are reading this and contemplating your own radio silence, I would emphasize that point over and over again. Take it to heart, as literally as possible. It's not that you are a lesser being; we cannot say for sure how the Gods choose whom they will speak to, but we can say that it is never about being an unworthy person. Know that it is not due to any lack of character or morals.

There is also solace in the knowledge that, in many ways, it is more honorable to hold faith in the face of divine silence than to believe only because the Gods bother you so much that you can't do otherwise. (There's a telling scene in the movie *Constantine* where the mortal main character—chosen for his psychic talents to be a demon-slayer—argues with the angel Gabriel. He contends that he should go to heaven because he is a believer; Gabriel says, "No. You *know*. That's different.") It's not that people who communicate more easily with Gods and spirits don't have their own mountains of faith to contend with—including faith in the benevolence of the Divine—but the initial mountain of faith in its very existence is in many ways a far greater struggle, and one could consider it more worthy to conquer.

It's also important for people who *do* have some kind of regular connection to the Holy Powers, especially if they didn't have to work hard for it, to internalize that point as well. The Yoga Sutras, which detail at some length the spiritual powers one can gain through the yogic disciplines, emphasize that while these powers indicate a certain level of spiritual attainment, they are largely an obstacle in one's path and a distraction from the real work of spirituality. The misinformed attitude that having a natural connection to the presence of the Holy Powers must be based on some kind of innate merit or worthiness is responsible not only for a great deal of insecurity on the part of those who aren't getting through, but also for a great deal of egotistical behavior on the part of those who are. Of course, this may only be a matter of time until the Gods decide that it's time for them to be publicly humbled, because they do love to set us up for a fall from pride. It's making sure that we drink the milk, you see.

One more reminder that can be stated about Divine Silence is that it does not go both ways. You may not be able to hear them, but they can certainly still hear you. Praying still counts, even in apparent isolation. They may or may not choose to reply directly, and not all the Gods will pay attention to you personally, but you can be assured that if you pray, Someone will hear. This, too, has been borne out by many thousands of years of experience. Our ancestors did not forget it, and we shouldn't either.

## Living In Mythic Time

The esteemed mythologist Joseph Campbell wrote that a myth was "...something that never happened but is always true." When we talk about myth, we trespass on concepts that are not easily comprehended fully by the human mind, which is used to linear time in which there is one concrete line of events that cannot be changed once it has happened, and one cannot switch to another world of possibilities. The first big question is whether myth is "true", as Joseph Campbell tried to poetically describe. Myth is not exactly fiction—in that it is not just a made-up story—and not exactly fact—in that it may not have literally happened in this linear-time plane—and not entirely metaphor, either. It is a story that describes a greater truth, a truth that is truer, so to speak, than our literal universe—a truth that need not have actually happened in order to be true. As such, the only way that it can come into our world is in the guise of a story.

No story is exact truth—we know that if we ask everyone involved in a particular event to write their perceptions of it, they will often write quite different tales. Personal perceptions are always skewed to the mind of the storyteller, which is why it is the nature of storytelling to be inexact when it comes to facts. However, a good story has the chance of bypassing fact and opening a door for that higher truth to enter the world; if it does this well enough to attract people and be passed on, it becomes myth.

Myths have different reasons for being, and some myths have several purposes. One purpose, for example, was to attempt to explain the working of the natural world. The involvement of a God/dess in the story was more than simply a way to assign divine responsibility to a natural occurrence. It is also testimony to the fact that when we ask great questions of the Universe, sometimes the Gods answer us, and their answer comes from their perspective which is not always the literal material truth that we perhaps expected. It is also testimony to how bound up their presence is with our lives.

Another purpose of myths is the ways that we tell each other about how we live in the world, including our fears and hopes and differing reactions to the same experience. This is where myths come into their archetypal aspect. Archetypes have been described metaphorically as many things, but I like to think of them as grooves in the Universe. Many of those grooves were made by Gods long before we existed to walk them. Others were made by Gods who had not yet connected with us, but when that connection was made, the strength of their energies in the mythic groove would highlight that situation and make it archetypal, and we would be inspired to write that myth—sometimes (though not always) starring them.

When something intense and life-changing happens to a human being, it leaves behind a residue. People who clean haunting out of houses have often run into the worst variety of that residue—a sort of "stain" on the atmosphere that is triggered like an old tape by the presence of humans and their life force, and runs its little movie of sorrow and despair and terror. There are more positive sorts of "stains", of course; for example, doing repeated magical workings or repeated psychic cleansings in a space can change its energetic nature, temporarily or permanently. This energy changing can apply to buildings, natural sites, objects, and even words and concepts. Intensity begins it, but repetition continues it—and it is repetition of the energetic act that creates permanent changes.

When something intense happens to a God, the same thing happens, but on a much grander scale. The energetically intense passage of a God through a series of circumstances causes more than a stain—it creates a kind of "groove" permanently carved into the Universe, a path that now has its own energy to carry something (energy, people, other Gods, etc.) from point A to point B. Images and items that are associated with that groove can carry a little of a its power, and can pull intent into that groove. Once a "package" of energy and intent gets into a groove, the groove itself will carry it to its natural end, without any additional energy from the spell-flinger. One could picture it as aiming your spell into a pinball channel, where it will be flung and dropped by forces beyond your control until it reaches its end.

To a certain extent, we walk unconsciously on these roads all the time, often many of them simultaneously. Sometimes we get stuck on one, living an archetype so deeply that walking away from it seems incomprehensible, but usually we inhabit several at once in a lighter manner, and the push-and-pull of our various mythic paths keeps any one from dominating our lives. It's a natural check-and-balance.

We may even be dimly aware of those grooves, especially when we take part in some social ritual designed to allow us to fully inhabit a mythical groove if only for a few hours, and then give us a push down enough of that path to make it one of our part-time permanent roads. Anyone who has ever gotten married with the big white wedding can probably understand what I'm talking about. One could call that the Hera/Juno groove, considering the historical and cultural development of that particular ceremony, and its focus on making the bride the center of attention. To take part in it with enthusiasm, whether you are the bride or the bridegroom, is to fully inhabit the first defining moment of that mythical groove. The unspoken idea behind the ceremony is that the couple will then be blessed with the positive aspects of that path for the rest of their marriage, a sort of shadow of that road. The unspoken fact is that they will also be plagued by many of the negative aspects of that myth as well—the jealousy, the struggle for power, the use of social inequalities as a weapon in that struggle—unless they are conscious enough to deliberately choose otherwise, and then to craft an alternate road that keeps them safely away from that groove. You can't choose just the good parts; you have to take the whole package, or nothing at all.

Once in a while you find someone who has been entirely swallowed by a single groove, doing nothing but living that archetype. This is a very difficult place to be in, and it can be rather unhealthy. This is someone who has been swallowed by that energy, and goes about embodying their role to the greatest extent that a human being can manage. The role seeps into every part of their personality, and they can become little more than that role in every part of their lives. While being a public figure seems to contribute greatly to this problem, there are also plenty of people who are doing it without any kind of public acclaim.

This is differentiated from the true avatar, who is simply a manifestation of a piece of the divinity's soul, and has no other karmic lessons, and fully spiritually prepared to do it cleanly. It is also differentiated from someone who has been given to life work to be a conscious doorway for the direct energy of a deity who is working closely with them. This can also be a very difficult thing, as the individual's will and personality is entirely sacrificed to the groove or to the divine role—but the key word there is sacrifice. Human doorways happen because it is necessary for the good of humanity for them to exist, and there is usually some sort of consent involved, even if it's not very well-informed consent, or it was made in an overawed state in the presence of Divinity. Sometimes sacrifices are necessary, because people need to see a living representation of that divine energy, and because its presence in a corporeal body gives the deity in question an open door through which to work change.

However, someone who has become subsumed into the energy of a groove rather than of a God/dess is in a somewhat worse position. First, there may not have been nearly the kind of active consent that occurs when a deity says, "I want to work through you, and this is how I will help you survive it and still have space for your own evolution." or something to that extent. For most groove-junkies, the process is more along the lines of an addiction than an active surrender. Second, for the human who periodically embodies the direct energy of a deity, the relationship with the deity can itself be a source of comfort and inspiration when things become difficult, and can provide more certainty in direction. The deity may also actively help their human doorway with the agonizing process of setting themselves aside in order to be a clean vessel; a groove-junkie must fumble their way through on their own, and it will be a lot harder for them to do it cleanly. That's why, as a spirit-worker, when I discern that someone is stuck in a groove to the point where they are losing themselves, I ask about the suitability of two choices: helping them to pry themselves out of it, or helping to facilitate their surrender to a deity who can guide and aid them—ideally the God who made or walked that road themselves—if the human being in question is absolutely invested in that road.

On a higher level, these mythic grooves are much more than just a bunch of roads, created accidentally or deliberately. They are part of the energy network in the Universe, the wires that express the rules about how the Universe works—and they change continually, because the Universe continues to change, no matter much we like to think of it as being static. They are the cosmic nervous system that carries the impulses from extremity to central hub to extremity again, and we—and the Gods—are the pulses, the energy signatures, that ride along them. This concept certainly isn't original to modern polytheists; the groove mechanism is alluded to in many ancient discussions of Words of Power—theurgic symbols that hook into a groove. One example is the Sumerian concept of the *me*, the magical words that described how to properly do anything—and that, when uttered, would automatically teach any person how to inhabit that task or role. (Supposedly the *me* were the property of the Gods, and they fought bitterly over who should be in charge of them.)

I should add, also, that there's no way to get away from mild, everyday interactions with those grooves, because there are so many of them. You're not supposed to avoid them; they exist for a good reason. The ideal is to have a variety of them in your life, and to learn to interact skillfully with them. (Rather like having people in your life. They can cause you trouble, but the answer is not to avoid them all.) Fortunately, part of learning how to be a polytheist is learning how to skillfully manage real spiritual diversity, and that skill can carry over into this area of existence as well.

Yet another purpose of myth is to attempt to explain the natures of the Gods themselves, by squeezing their vast energies through the filter of human experience. While we and they are capable of having similar experiences, one must not assume that by reading the human stories of their activities, we are able to fully comprehend them. Every deity is, by definition, seen through a human lens. We cannot connect with them without distorting who and what they are, because we are what we are, and that includes the filter of our human nature. Our tales about them have more to do with us and our relationship with them than they have to do with their essential nature when we are not around and interacting with them. While we should not pretend that our filtered stories exactly describe the Gods as the Universe sees them, they are what we have to work with. Myths also need to be both simple and complex, easy to remember so that they can be passed down to one's descendants, and with enough depth and layers that they will help to shape the world view of the future. (It's been pointed out that mythic time very much resembles the way that time passes in dreams, and considering that dreams—and the imagination centers of the mind—are common triggers that the Gods use to communicate with us, this makes a good deal of sense.)

For that matter, yet another purpose for myths is that they are good and entertaining stories, the blockbuster fiction of each era. If they don't hold an audience's interest, they will be forgotten, and it is the job of the priest or bard or skald to do their deity honor by making sure that this doesn't happen. We must never forget the need of human beings to entertain each other with a good story, and to change that story if the original was not entertaining enough. Of course, considering that there are also deities whose job it is to oversee the storytelling process, and that the truest myths ring out and touch people in a way that bowdlerized versions often don't, it's possible that every part of the myth-creation process is affected by the tweaking of our Gods.

When we deal with Gods and their natures, we have to deal with the fact that they do not exist in the same linear time-scale that we do. Some of them have linear myths that follow them throughout their lives; others have no real "stories" that we have retained records of, but simply seem to appear as cameos in the myths of other Gods. Some even have conflicting myths, or share myths with other God/desses, a situation that makes us throw up our hands in frustration when we try to compare their stories to our own very linear experience of time.

For us, our lives are more marked by Doing than Being. It is not that we cannot experience pure Being—and experiencing that state is certainly part of the spiritual goals and practices of many religious traditions—but by the nature of our world and our existence, Doing is very important to us, and we mark the passing of Time by the effects that the physical world has on us and how those affect what we Do. While we remember Being in different states in the past, those are—in most cases—memories, while for the Gods those moments are just as real to them as the present moment, and they can become the being who is living that moment again at any time.

This is especially true for the "formative" experiences in their lives, the ones that shaped their natures and made them what they are. Formative experiences—and especially traumatic ones—are important in shaping who we are as well; I do not mean to discount that, but it is never as literal for us as it is for a deity who is of a more monolithic nature than we are. If we go through a strongly shaping—and perhaps shattering—experience, we may say that some part of us is still there, living and reliving that experience and never getting away from it. However, when we say that, we mean it metaphorically. For a deity, this is quite literal. Some aspect of them is formed in that moment, and that aspect can be called upon, and if they appear they will be just as the God or Goddess was in that formative moment, even if that moment is far in the past. They will be aware to some extent of the future divine self that you are familiar with, because the future—while it is variable and not set—is more known to them than it is to us.

To use an example: If I call upon Aphrodite the mourning lover of Adonis and she graces me with her presence, I will get Aphrodite as she was in that moment, the moment where her mortal lover died and passed beyond her reach forever, and she realized the full consequences of what it was to invest not just your time and affection but your whole heart into a being who lived on such a different plane of experience from you that there could be no end to the story but tragedy. My presence, and my understanding of her myth as having moved on through the mourning and come back to herself eventually, will anchor her to that possible future rather than other possible futures (where, for example, she might slay herself from grief), but she will be aware of that future as a premonition coming through her own higher self rather than a part of herself as certain as the moment she stands in. And yet if it is necessary for some reason, she can just as quickly become that future Aphrodite who has passed through mourning and regained her golden glow.

If I call upon Sigyn—the second wife of the Norse trickster god Loki and the goddess of compassion and endurance in Northern Tradition Paganism—as her aspect as the blithe child bride, if she comes she will exist in that moment, and act and react from that moment. My presence will anchor her to a future where she must see her children destroyed and her husband imprisoned and tortured for hundreds of years, and where she must stay by him, starve with him, and comfort him for all that time until he is released. That future will be a shadow that lies over the innocent child bride, and she will not be unaware of it, but it will not be her reality at that moment. Should I call upon her as the Mourning Mother trapped in the cave with her suffering husband bound with their slain son's intestines, if she comes it will be in the agony of that moment as well. Because I know that they will eventually be freed, there will be the echo of hope hanging over the terrible grief she carries. However, even if she were to come as the Sigyn who is now free to live in a small cottage in Jotunheim with her husband, she could be transported back to that moment if it was necessary for our interactions—and it would not be "the past", it would be What Is Happening Now. It's a difficult concept for us to understand and follow, but I think it is enough that we know it exists.

As you can imagine, the "mythic moments" are different for a more humanlike aspect of deity than they are for that deity's higher self. The more personal and humanlike aspects experience those moments with much more intensity; they are utterly immersed in each one as it happens to them. The higher self of a deity is a little more distanced from the intensity, and has integrated those moments more fully into their being.

In addition, since nonlinear time also means that separate myths can exist for separate possibilities—one story for the Goddess who took this direction, another for the same Goddess who made a different choice—this entails accepting that more than one myth "can have happened" in some way, at some point, in some fold of the Universe. Was Persephone raped and carried off by Hades, or did Persephone go down willingly of her own accord because she heard the ghosts whispering and wanted to help them? Either myth may be true, and "may have happened" in alternate paradigms, with both myths coming together at the point where Persephone takes the hand of Hades and becomes Queen of the Underworld and Wise Counselor of the Dead.

This concept also explains the hundreds—perhaps thousands—of creation myths in existence. It is possible, in mythic time, that they all happened in different folds of the Universe and then came together synchronously into one blossoming Existence. We are used to the idea of time being one line of things that definitely happened, splitting into a tree of possibilities in front of us, of which we are only going to take one and the others will fall away into nonexistence. It's harder for us to imagine the past as a spreading tree of alternate pasts behind us, all of which have merged into our present; and of course the tree in front of us is another set of possibilities that branch off into existences that will all actually have happened when they, too, merge into another key present moment. However, meditating on this concept of time and consequence may bring us a little closer to understanding the worlds of the Gods.

Mythic time perception can also vary depending on where one was raised. I was born and raised in a modern western culture, and my birth culture focuses very strongly on seeing everything in linear time. In contrast, many (though not all) aboriginal cultures see time very differently. Some linguists claim that the language of one's upbringing changes how one thinks about time, and growing up, for example, with a language such as that of the Hopi Indians—which has no tenses for past or present or future, and which describes a conception of time that is circular and cyclical rather than linear—would completely change someone's ability to comprehend the non-linear time of the Gods without confusion. When we consider the paradox of mythic time versus linear time, we must remember that the Indo-European-derived language in which this book is written, and which many of the people reading it will have grown up speaking, and the subsequent worldview that it describes, is hardly the way that all human beings think or have ever thought about time. Once we account for that, the gulf between mythic and linear time becomes a little less vast. It's something for those of us with the handicap of a modern western upbringing to think about, and perhaps strive toward.

Dementia aside, one of the reasons that it is normal for the very old to remember their younger days with sudden vividness, and sometimes feel as if they are experiencing them again, is partially due to the fact that getting closer to Death distorts linear time for you on a spiritual level. It brings you closer to the world of Spirit, and of the Gods, where all points on the wheel are, if not equally accessible, certainly more accessible and closer to the heart of your being than simply the present moment. For that matter, the main point of religious practices that focus on learning to Be rather than simply to Do is because they bring one closer to divine mythic time, and thus to the Gods themselves.

Some people might say that we, too, live in non-linear time, but we aren't aware of it—or we deliberately ignore it because it is too confusing to contemplate. This calls in the possibility of our past lives, and which parts of our soul reincarnate or stay to be called upon or dissolve into the Universe, which is a different discussion. Mostly, we deal with the concept of mythic time by trying to ignore it. However, if we are going to try to understand our Gods to the best of our mortal abilities, it behooves us to remember, again and again, that they live much looser in the flow of Happening, and that to attempt to box them into discrete causal events that draw hard lines between "who they were then" and "who they are now" is an exercise in futility.

## Gender, Sex, and Gods

Throughout the Old Testament, YHWH made it clear that he was male, and his followers did not question that until modern times, when some Christian churches began to refer to God as a genderless being. Of course, the conception of the Hebrews of their male patron deity—one of many but the One who had chosen them—and the conception of modern Christians of a deity who was assumed to be the ultimate transcendent Power, are necessarily very different. It is true and unarguable that the Architect of the Universe is beyond gender; it's just not necessarily the case from the view of a polytheist that YHWH is any more a representative embodiment of that force than any other deity. Given this, I am quite convinced that YHWH is male, just as I am quite convinced that Inanna is female. (There's also the difficult possibility that when a member of the Abrahamic faiths calls on "God", it's not always YHWH who answers, but most people can't tell.)

By being polytheistic, we sidestep all the issues that women in Abrahamic religions endure with regard to a lack of models of the Divine Feminine. However, what's even better is that we have models beyond that. When the Neo-Pagan movement began back in the 1960s, it started largely with Wicca, which is a duotheistic initiatory mystery religion that leans heavily on the concept of heterosexual polarity—a male God and female Goddess in eternal romantic or mother-son relationship. The emphasis on sacred polarity, while it was probably an incredible breath of fresh air to people who grew up with nothing but a male god to look to, was still limited enough that a twenty-year war raged among early Wiccan covens about whether gay men and lesbians should be allowed into their ranks, and if so, whether they should be forced to enact ritual only in the traditional heterosexually-paired roles.

As Neo-Paganism spread and diversified, however—and especially as Pagans began to embrace polytheism rather than duotheism—it became clear that the ancient Gods came in many genders and many sexual preferences, a wide spectrum rather than a narrow pairing. There were extremely traditionally female Goddesses and extremely traditionally male Gods; there were masculine Goddesses and feminine Gods; there were outright bi-gendered deities (and ones that switched back and forth). There were as many variations as there are human beings, when those human beings are allowed to express themselves and their genders freely in open societies.

To those who first objected to a monochromatic metaphorical-divine-gender flag, a bi-colored one must have seemed like a huge improvement—and an enormous first step. However, the rainbow-watercolors of pantheism and the wildly varying patchwork of polytheism were rather bewildering to them. While some Pagan groups—namely the Wiccan and Wiccan-derived varieties—do still concentrate on a Divine Feminine and Divine Masculine, the polytheistic worldview is too diverse for that. A Goddess may be female, but she may also express her femininity in a way that is wildly different from another Goddess—and in fact her essence may be more similar to a male deity who has the same job that she does. It makes more sense for the polytheist looking for an example of divine gender to follow to examine the "gender performance", if you will, of a number of deities and then choose the one(s) most like their own, or like their ideal.

Still, given this, there are some deities who take it on themselves to initiate men and women into the biologically gendered mysteries, and these Gods and Goddesses might be considered the most "essentially" feminine or masculine. Since we are all born of the fruit of those mysteries—every one of us is the product of heterosexual intercourse, pregnancy, and birth—and because all of the nourishing food that we eat is also a product of that procreative fertility, some deities embody that absolute ends-of-spectrum procreative biological reality. Some also embody femaleness or maleness in-and-of itself, in its essential purity, without being in a pairing of polarity. (These are often "virgin" or permanently unpaired deities, like Artemis.) Our patchwork quilt is such that every permutation of gender, linked to the physical body or not, has a divine embodiment somewhere.

The gender of Gods in relation to our own genders is also an exercise in diversity. Even the most male-preferring of Gods has a few female followers; the most woman-preferring of Goddesses has some men devoted to her (such as the men who were documented followers of Artemis). Most Gods and Goddesses tend to choose far more often on the basis of personality affinity rather than bodily configuration. This doesn't mean that specific bodily configuration can't get you extra affinity points, especially if you are looking at a deity whose personal mysteries include the biological mysteries of a particular physical configuration (for example, Baphomet, who is deeply bound up with the bodily experience of mixed physical gender attributes in any combination, and can be expected to respond to any intersex or transgendered person who has the courage to approach). However, it seems to be a guarantee that even those God/desses will accept someone who is not of that bodily configuration. Perhaps they are able to take on that configuration on an energy-body level—something which the Gods definitely recognize as much more significant than we do—or perhaps there is some other affinity of personality or life-sphere that we don't happen to see. Gods are not so monolithic of nature that they cannot make exceptions out of some version of divine love.

When it comes to sex, it's clear that most of our Gods are sexual. Some of them are quite literally Gods of sex. A few, such as Hestia or Athena, are sexual renunciates, but even these are such because there is a power in consciously rerouting any strong energy, not because sex is wrong or even "less" in the value-scale of activities and energies. Many polytheistic religions have sexual metaphors for the creation of the world, or graphically sexual creation myths. Sex, for us, is something wonderful and sacred, like eating and nourishment, which can be chosen or rerouted into other paths, as people wish. Sex is something that both Nature and our Gods do, wildly and joyously and profligately, with as many different patterns and styles as we ourselves may favor. Our Gods have sex to create children, or create worlds, or to express joy, or power, or divine love.

Once in a great while, in rare circumstances, the Gods may bless their worshipers with sex. This can be as simple as blessing a couple with particularly wonderful energy in the midst of the act, or as complex as offering to have sexual congress of some kind with a worshiper. The experience of this latter situation will vary depending on the level of human-divine spiritual connection; some worshipers have simply had vague but moving masturbatory experiences with a strong sense of the presence of that God or Goddess, and others have had full-sensory experiences with a deity and their own energy body. One of the Cosmic Laws that we are sure of, however, is that sexual congress with a deity must be consented to. There may be, however, a good deal of grey area when it comes to conscious and unconscious consent—it has been documented more than once among people who compare these experiences that some (not all) Gods will respond to one's repressed desire rather than one's spoken refutation, sometimes forcefully. This is even rarer, though, and if every part of you is against the idea, they will not force it on you.

Another Cosmic Law of which we are even more sure is that no deity can take you in marriage unless you consent, wholly and willingly. The phenomenon of the "god-spouse" is lightly touched on in the Relationships chapter, but it can be seen primarily as a full-time dedication to a specific God as part of an intensely personal devotional path. The path of the Pagan god-spouse has been compared to the Hindu concept of *bhakti*—worshiping a deity through strong personal romantic love, of the sort that people usually only think about in relation to other human beings. It is vaguely like the Christian "Bride of Christ" idea, but far more personal, and can include a very sexual and passionate way of relating. However, others may have less committed but no less ecstatic sexual encounters with a number of Gods over their lifetimes.

Some Pagan traditions also practice giving sexual energy as an offering to Gods and spirits. This can involve one or more people raising sexual energy in themselves and releasing it to the honored entity, either in ritual or just as an act of general goodwill. It's not uncommon for them to feel a sense of presence as they accomplish the act, and on rare occasions it can lead to the deity getting involved themselves. In addition to this, some very rare humans are called to the job of *qadishtu*, which (for those who haven't heard of it) is essentially hands-on sex therapy in sacred space, usually a temple, under the aegis of whichever love or sex deity is invoked to help with the work. It is a very selfless service job, and one which is most definitely not for everyone, as the ego must be kept very much out of it.

No matter what the sex act, there is probably a legend somewhere about a deity who did it, or its ancient equivalent, and will probably approve of you doing it as well. However, as we've said before, even deities are subject to the laws of consequence, and you even more so. Some sex acts—rape, for instance—may be mythically appropriate to certain circumstances which you are not engaged in, and probably never will be, so in your case the act will most certainly have a negative return for you. Sexual ethics need to be worked out with an eye to where you are now, not the fantasy world that you wish you were in. If you are in need of help, asking Gods of rules and justice can help you work out what it right. Again, that's why we are polytheists—no one deity has all the answers, but if you honor more than one, you get enough perspectives to balance everything out.

## Death and Her Options

People tend to email me on a regular basis and ask questions about Pagan religion, and one of the biggest questions they ask—indeed, one of the biggest questions of all—is "What happens when we die?" Most religions have limited answers to that question. In fact, most have only two options: Something Good or Something Bad. A few have only one answer. It's one-size-fits-all, or two-sizes-should-fit-most.

As you might expect from a religion that values diversity so strongly and eschews the Good/Bad binary equally intensely, death in our purview is not so simple a concept. First, there's the underlying idea that death is not inherently bad or evil in and of itself. There's no question that it can cause grief, but grief is also an inherent and sacred part of experiencing this cycle of life. Death is simply an inevitability. We might fight it to a standstill for a particular life's moment, but sooner or later it will come anyway ... and that does not have to be seen as a bad thing.

Where do our souls go when we die? That depends ... on a lot of different variables. Options can include:

❖ Reincarnation. It is part of our world view on Death, but not necessarily the central fact of it, as it could be considered in Hinduism. Some people walking on the earth today have lived many other lives in bodies on this earth. Some people are here for the first time. Some will never live more than one life here before going on to something else. There can also be a large gap (in our time, remember that time is not linear for the Gods) between one incarnation and the next. Some theologies posit that reincarnation happens mostly or entirely down genetic bloodlines. While I agree that this can happen, I am not sold on it being an across-the-board situation, being that reincarnation memories can take place across the world in many different genetic groups. However, some people who hold the ancestral-reincarnation as an absolute be-all and end-all believe that one can incarnate as the ancestors of one's future descendants, so if someone with entirely European bloodlines had a series of past lives in Asia, perhaps they are incarnating the lives of the ancestors of some Asian-descended person who will eventually breed with one of their European-descended descendants, and bind the two lines together. It's an interesting theory, but currently hard to prove.

- ❖ Going to live with (or perhaps become one with) one's patron deity, or some deity that chooses to take you to their breast when you go. Some people look forward to serving their Gods in person someday; others hope to be allowed to bask in their presence or run about in their house like children. Some choose to merge with their deity entirely. Since the Gods are vastly larger than human, the human characteristics are entirely subsumed.

- ❖ Going to some cultural-cosmological Underworld. There are many of them, all with different styles and characteristics, but usually there is one deity in charge of who comes and goes. Some ancient cultures—such as the Greeks—had one Underworld that took everyone, with different areas in it. Others had several separate underworlds; the Norse/Germanic peoples had Valhalla and Sessrumnir (for warriors who died in battle), Aegirheim (for those drowned at sea) and Helheim (for everyone else). Some cosmologies, like many of the Afro-Caribbean ones, were (and are) quite vague on where people went after death. I count the Christian afterworld as part of this group, just another cultural post-life lodging point.

- ❖ Going to be with one's ancestors, in a sort of "ancestral village". This may happen for people who are fairly genetically homogenous, and very tied to their ancestral traditions.

- ❖ Becoming one with the spirit of a particular place. Some human spirits meld, over time, with land-spirits, and become guardians of certain areas.

- ❖ Dissolving and becoming one with the Universe. We know that it happens to some people, but we're not sure why or how often. Again, in my world this is not the sign of being more evolved. It may be a last-ditch solution for a very damaged soul that has not found healing any other way.

- ❖ And, of course, there is the option of getting stuck here on this plane as a wandering ghost, but that is always a temporary situation. Ghosts are able to maintain themselves on this plane by feeding off of ambient energy (including terrified people), but eventually they begin to fade. Either they go off to one of the aforementioned places, or they become one with the land-spirit of wherever they are (not uncommon for ghosts who are bound to one place by their love of it), or in very rare cases they hitch along as a "rider" on the soul of a living person. Note the "very rare", though, before you start thinking about your friends and jumping to conclusions.

How do you know where you'll go? You probably don't, unless you have a relationship with a specific deity and they have assured you that it is taken care of—you'll go to their house or cultural Underworld. Reincarnation is common, but not universal; going to one's ancestral village is also common all over the world, although less so in modern populations with hugely eclectic ancestry. But any of these options could happen, and probably a few that I haven't thought of.

The big question is: how is it decided? After being asked this question for years, I finally decided to find out as surely as I could. Since I belong to a Death Goddess, and have worked with half a dozen other death deities, and have spent a lot of time sending lost dead people on to wherever they needed to go, I asked to be shown how it is decided ... in some way other than my immediate death, of course. It was granted, and I watched the next time I helped a dead soul on her way ... and the next, and the next. What I can tell you is this: At the moment of your death, many decisions are suddenly made for you. Some of them may have been made beforehand, but there was a definite sense of "summing up" in the moment. The idea of death as "the reckoning" is not merely a Christian phenomenon.

At that moment, Someone took over and took charge of the soul as it was passing. In some cases, it may have been Someone that the soul had already been involved with; in other cases the Someone seemed to simply step forward and take charge. Sometimes this was a death deity, and sometimes a spirit that I could not identify, exactly. The most appropriate option for that soul was decided, based not on anything punitive that I could see, but on what would be best for their evolution—and, sometimes, their need for healing. Other variables included outstanding promises and obligations—to friends and loved ones, to ancestral ties, to Gods and spirits. And, yes, lessons to be learned were in there as well. With all the foresight and knowledge available to that Someone, including the knowledge gained by understanding nonlinear time and the huge array of potential circumstances in the web of all Life, the absolute best decision is made as to where that soul should go. The next decision to be made—in a split second thereafter—was about who should be the first to meet them when they come over. God or mortal soul? It's all done with an awe-inspiring amount of love, no matter who they were, or what they did, or how they died.

That's something that I've noticed about Death Gods in general—they tend to be rather stern and implacable toward the still-living (perhaps because their spiritual task for us is to be the force that says No), but they are incredibly tender toward the Dead who are their charges. Once we have passed over, we get to see their immense compassion. Granted, I've never watched the passing over of a mass murderer, but I'm quite certain that they would be received with the same clean compassion. There is nothing malicious or punitive there.

I've also seen the parts of the various Underworlds where people suffer. The Christian Hell (which I admit I have never seen or dealt with) supposedly is a place entirely of punishment, but even ancient Pagan underworlds sometimes had sections where people who had done bad things would be sent to endure torments. The first one that I saw up close was Nastrond, the hall in Helheim where dead souls lie screaming under the dripping fangs of vipers. I stared in horror, and then the Death Goddess who owns both me and that realm pointed out that the door was not locked, and that they could leave at any time. I realized with a start that sometimes human souls need a place to work things out—guilt, remorse, pain—and this is one of the options that they can choose. When they have finished with it, they will leave.

Death, in our world view, is not the simple black-and-white concept that it is in many other religions. It is not evil, and it is not the door to some unchanging eternity. Even the options that seem eternally changing are not, according to She who was there during my own near-death experience. Eventually, everything moves on again. Even the souls who become one with the Universe, completely dissolving into Nothingness. After all, She pointed out, where did I think the new souls came from? Everything, in our Universe, is a cycle ... with no beginning, and never ending. That's the most obvious Mystery of all.

## Divination: Knowing What Is Knowable

One of the customs that makes Neo-Pagan theology so different from most other mainstream religions is our practice of ritual and religious divination. Fortunetelling can also be done for completely secular purposes—and often is, sometimes by the same people who do religious community divination, because the skills are the same and they want to help support themselves in the rest of their life—but specifically religious divining has been done for thousands of years. In secular divination, the diviner seeks to tap into the "cosmic library" regarding one person's fate or current situation, with or without the aid of spirits. In religious divination, the Gods themselves are specifically asked to reveal the answer to a situation, usually relating to their worship or their worshipers. It is assumed that they will have an opinion on the matter, and that their opinion will probably be based on a broader and more informed perspective than our own.

Many mainstream religions eschew divination, with the reasoning that it "steals God's powers". (In other mainstream traditions, the objection is that it comes from the Devil—which is irrelevant to our world view—or that it shows a lack of faith because if God wanted to tell you, God would be direct, which we also believe is not necessarily true.) In Pagan traditions, divination has been accepted in ways that range from enthusiastic to suspicious, but even in the traditions that suspect it, the validity of the practice is not suspicious so much as the skill and honesty of the practitioners.

In the minority of Pagan groups who eschew divination for religious purposes, their objection seems to stem from a perception of the diviners themselves as being highly likely to insert their own message instead of the will of the Divine, and an inability of the watching clergy and congregation to discern the diviner's skill and clarity. This is a valid fear—and one which is dealt with in the aforementioned by myself and Kenaz Filan on talking to the spirits—but divination as a spiritual practice is deeply entwined with Pagan religious history, and we know it. Temples almost always had professional diviners, and before that tribal priests and shamans did the job for their people, figuring out who could be called upon for aid and who should be propitiated. Auguries and omens were a means by which our Gods communicated with their worshipers, as was trance mediumship.

Kings, generals, and chieftains consulted the most famous oracles, who became famous largely due to their accuracy.

Those of us who have performed religious divination know that the idea of "stealing divine powers" is ludicrous. We *can't* steal divine powers. It's not possible, and the idea itself is an immense act of hubris. We are only allowed to see what the Holy Powers allow us to see, and they are absolutely capable of stepping in and shutting down our perceptions, or erecting a sudden wall between us and our desired information. In many divination systems there is even a specific sign or symbol which means "Sorry, you don't get to know that." When this comes up in a reading, I take it as the Holy Powers saying, "This will be much more meaningful to you if you figure it out yourself, rather than just hearing it come out of the mouth of some diviner." It might also be "There's a long-term good reason why you don't get to know that yet, and to explain the reason would be to give too much away."

Divination is no more stealing divine power than, say, a microscope might be. We can't see microbes with our physical eyes, and before we knew how to look at them, we were much more likely to be killed by them. Most of us would not agree that microscopes are "cheating" and that we should all be trying to live with only the information we can gather with our ordinary, unassisted senses, especially when it comes to saving people's lives. Similarly, divination is just another kind of technology, and like all technologies, the Gods are quite skilled at helping or blocking results.

Believing in and using divination does throw a different slant on our religious beliefs, however. While I am sure that all Pagan polytheists would agree that there is a great deal about the Gods and spirits that we cannot comprehend, and that some of those mysteries will probably remain mysteries forever, the presence of divination does increase the horizons of what we actually do consider to be knowable. We might ask questions about the best spiritual or mundane direction of a seeker, or the best action in a difficult situation, or what Gods or spirits that seeker should be consulting, and what those spirits might want of them. Religious divination tends to be less about love life or career, the top subjects for secular readers, and more about spiritual life direction. It can be a useful skill for a clergyperson who does pastoral counseling; when it is done properly, it can give insight into potential paths that the counselor might not have figured out on their own. It can also ask about deities themselves—what they might want, how they work in the world, what their nature might be. It is a good way for the Gods to communicate with people who don't have the right wiring to consistently hear the voices of ethereal beings, but need a specific message given to them anyway.

Divination is practiced in non-western polytheistic religions as well; Hindu temples never stopped having diviners, and Vedic astrology directs the lives of a sizeable percentage of India. Buddhism also has a variety of divination methods associated with it; while "pure" Buddhism is not technically polytheist at all (and actually has a number of early writings that speak out against divination), it merged with the original polytheistic religions everywhere it settled, and adopted their pantheons, their divinatory methods, and the assumption of their people that the new priests would offer this service as well. Later Buddhist writings explored arguments justifying divination in order to make theological peace with this adopted practice, and it is still customary in most of Buddhist Asia.

Even the most divination-resistant faiths have some kind of practice of attempting to speak to the divine forces, if only through prayer. One could consider religious divination as a form of highly structured prayer, with the structure set up in such a way as to make it as effective as possible for the Holy Powers to get through any messages they may have for us. After all, we can't make them talk; nor can we force the Akashic Records (or whatever you want to call it) to open for us merely because we demand it. If we consider the information that is given to us through divining—whether about our own lives or about the nature and desires of the Gods—to be a gift to us that is only given if it would be in the long-term best interest to do so, then we will not fall into any traps of hubris. However, as the man who first looked through a microscope discovered, what *can* be known is much, much more than we ever expected.

All theological discussion of divination eventually ends with the question of Fate, and usually people insist on asking either/or, black-and-white questions about whether we are all destined to lockstep through our lives with no free will, or whether there is no such thing as fate. As usual—and with what you've learned about a polytheistic worldview so far, you should be expecting this answer—it's not that simple, and there is no one answer that works for everyone. As far as we can tell, everyone destiny—and the amount of "destiny" one has—is very individual. Some people are allowed to mess around, make all their own choices, and rack up their own consequences; they are truly the captain of their own ships, for better or for worse. Some people have very strong destinies which will drag them, kicking and screaming if necessary, down a specific path to a set end. Most people, however, are somewhere in the middle; there are particular lessons that they will be made to learn, others that will simply be offered (sometimes repeatedly) in the hopes that they will willingly take them on, and a great deal of free will to screw up in between.

How does one find out what sort of destiny you have? Well, for thousands of years, and currently in many places in the world, one finds out through divination. (Astrology is particularly good at giving a general picture of one's destiny, or lack of it.) And, as any diviner will tell you, people with a strong destiny spend a great deal of time complaining about how little free will they have, and people who are here to make their own choices spend a great deal of time complaining about how they wish they knew what they were supposed to be doing. Even with all the information that the Gods are willing to give us, we still aren't satisfied ... and perhaps that is one of the most important lessons of all.

# Epilogue:
# Living In the World, Honoring The Worlds

> But above all
> Always above all else:
> How does one act
> If one believes what you say?
> Above all: how does one act?
> – Bertold Brecht, *The Doubter*

All this theorizing simply brings us to the final point: how do we act if we believe all this? It's fine to theorize about it, but what does the ordinary practice look like? I tried to explain, once, to a friend who had grown up Catholic, what it was like to have a number of powers to whom one made offerings and prayers, and the process of discerning who to call on for what problem, should you wish to implore divine aid. My friend listened with eyebrows raised and said, "That sounds exactly like my old Catholic grandmother with all her saints! Pray to Saint This for that, Saint That for this!" We both had to laugh—while Catholicism is not polytheistic per se, "folk" Catholicism ends up being remarkably similar to polytheistic practice, and indeed replaced the European polytheism that it nearly wiped out. This practice was even more distinct in the merging of the religions of African slaves with Catholic masters, and the African-diaspora faiths that resulted where the *lwa* or *orisha* are both embodiments of Catholic saints and of African Gods and ancestors as well.

As with all things religious, it depends a lot on how holistically you involve your faith with your life. For people of any faith who simply go to occasional ritual or service, perhaps keep a few cultural customs out of habit, and possibly remember their faith in times of great crisis or difficult ethical decision, but otherwise keep it largely out of their life ... well, they probably look more like each other than someone who is devoutly religious in any faith. Living a life that is fully imbued with polytheistic religion means a life, ideally, of mindfulness. Each thing that is done is under the aegis of some Power, and one can choose to call upon that power for a chance at deepening the experience of that activity. To me, when I get up and head sleepily to the bathroom, my toilet is a small iteration of the great well of Hvergelmir in Norse mythology, at the base of the World Tree where the great dragon Nidhogg devours corpses and transforms them into the compost that fertilizes the World Tree itself. In this mythology, the swirl of archetypes conflates roots, compost, fertilizer, rotting down, all that one wants to get rid of, the mouth of the dragon, and the great swirling well. My experience of relieving myself, and my momentary interaction with water and my septic system, is a microcosm of that myth and that divine force. Someone else might see it as a different mythic archetype, but the point remains. By connecting the two in my mind, I partake of a synchronous connection that is already there, and touch the being of the Great Dragon for just a moment.

I've deliberately used a small and often-despised routine as a way to show how polytheistic and mythic connections can be made, but the idea can be repeated with any ordinary function. Every time I say a few words to a deity of agriculture before I eat my food, I partake of that connection, if only in a small way. If I care enough about that deity to invoke their name before I eat, I care enough to discern their values, and that brings me around to changing what it is that I am actually eating, both as a nod to their wisdom on the matter and as a way to make that act more worthy of their blessing. There is no activity in life that cannot be treated in this way, if you try.

When I began writing this book, I asked many of my fellow polytheists to think up questions for me. I asked them what they would have wanted to know in the beginning, when they were exploring this kind of faith and didn't know anything about it, except that other sorts of faiths looked down on it as superstitious and ridiculous, perhaps not even "real" religion. They came through for me, and indeed, the framework of that long list of questions became the foundation for this book. However, after I'd delineated and wrestled with issues of origin, worldview, and morality, there were still two questions to which I had no definitive answer, and to which no specific polytheistic denomination has official answers, either. The first of these questions was familiar to seekers of any faith; it was often accompanied by that particular frustrated disappointment that occurs when one changes faiths and hopes for a better answer than they got from the last one, only to find that no one has a more satisfying answer.

It was the question of why, if someone loves the Gods and spirits, and does their best to worship them, work with them, and honor them, their life would not be made any easier. Did our Gods not have the power to help us with an easier life, it was asked, or are they not willing to do so? What is the point of religious worship if the circumstances of my life are still miserable?

We are hardly the first people to ask this question, and we will hardly be the last ones. The short answer is, of course, is that no amount of religious devotion will create an easy life, and unlike some religions, we must be clear about that. The point of life is not to be easy, but to be rewarding; the point of living on the material plane is not to be effortless but to be strongly experiential. However, the key to understanding this conundrum is in understanding the effects of getting close to the Gods and spirits in any way.

Spirit-workers—people of any tradition who work with multiple deities and spirits as part of a helping profession—have often commented on the interesting spiritual effect of bringing the Gods and spirits more directly into one's life. The most obvious—and difficult—effect is a kind of spiritual radiation that permeates an area and changes the randomness factor, making everything less random and raising the frequency of synchronicity. (One can hardly call it coincidence; in fact when the frequency and quality of coincidences reach ridiculous proportions, it's usually a sign that Gods and/or spirits are involved and there has ceased to be any sort of coincidence at all—it's all synchronicity.) Some scientists are now referring to a space where there is less random chance and more synchronicity as "ordered space". The Gods and spirits use the manipulation of synchronicity as a way to make things happen in our world, and their presence in our rituals, our devotions, and our lives releases a wave of ordered space into our auras and circumstances. Ordered space can also cling to a god-touched person, a long-time priest or priestess or spirit-worker or shaman, or a sacred site; touching them can bring on a smaller version of the kind of ordered space brought by the Gods and spirits that permeate them.

Another law that we as Neo-Pagan polytheists see as valid is the concept that what we do comes back to us. It is very rarely as neat as the Wiccan "Threefold Law"—that what one does comes back three times, which is difficult to quantify in real life and probably a poetic exaggeration—but we do acknowledge that it happens, even if it is delayed long enough or is obscure enough that we don't recognize it as an effect of our actions when it hits us. We don't see this as a bad thing; one reaps what one sows, in the way that the Universe deems most appropriate to your further education in this lifetime. The process of returning circumstances itself is dependent upon synchronicity, as it utilizes cascades of circumstance to happen at all. This means that ordered space has the singular effect of making that process more efficient; in other words, it speeds up your return on your actions. This is effectively being under more ferocious spiritual scrutiny; instead of being able to get away with your mistakes until it has been long enough that you don't make any conscious connection when the consequence comes around, you get to experience a much quicker return that is hard to ignore.

What this means for us as ordinary people is that the further you get down the path you're supposed to walk, the more synchronicity and less randomness there will be in your life. Patterns begin to emerge that had not resolved before. It's not mysterious—it's a natural phenomenon, and our Gods are both cause and guides to the process. However, it also means that stepping onto the path—consciously or otherwise—and then stepping back off due to fear, poor judgment, or just being an imperfect human creature can bring a greater amount of chaos into our lives than we would have had otherwise. Once the synchronicity is turned up, even just a little bit, we can't turn back. Is it worth it? In my experience, yes. It is worth every limit placed on our choices, because it brings us closer to the heart of reality.

In addition, some of us need to walk difficult patterns, for a variety of reasons. Sometimes it's because our souls have specific lessons that must be learned, and our particular personalities guarantee that we won't learn them the easy way. Sometimes it's bigger than our own personal path—*someone* has to walk that road, because it is necessary to the Universe, and we unconsciously volunteer because of our choices, or we are actively chosen by the Holy Powers because we happen to be some combination of karmically available and best suited to survive the task. When this happens—when we are taken by the Holy Powers to walk a path that might not otherwise have been our own personal path—our thread, as it were, is tied to that of a larger and more impersonal one, and our own destiny is subsumed into that wider path. This can come at great cost to us, but we still have at least one choice left. We can do our best to figure out how that larger path is best walked, or we can give up and fail out. In a case like this, the hard parts aren't necessarily because someone is doing it wrong. They may be endemic to the larger, more difficult road, and no one gets to the end of it without experiencing them.

That goes for the Gods, too. After all, don't they have their myths with trials and pitfalls that they must endure? This knowledge can sustain us when we feel that we are walking larger and more painful destinies that we didn't choose, when we are placed deliberately into those grooves in the Universe and we know that in this case, at least, there is no way out but through.

We can take comfort that our Gods were here before us, and they, too, are keenly aware of what we are going through. That's why, when you are going down one of those painful grooves, you have the right to call upon any deity who has also walked that road—not to rescue you, but to help you to find the strength to find your way through. For that matter, the road may also have been walked by other human beings who have now passed on, and they, too, can give comfort and succor. Don't be afraid to ask for help in these cases. After all, if it is in the best interest of the Universe that someone walks this road, then it also benefits the Gods and spirits, so if you're going to have to do it anyway you might as well exercise your right to ask for aid.

Remember, too, that awareness of their presences and their aid is often blocked by sorrow and anger, so it may be that the hardest times are when you may feel the most alone. Since we don't believe that our Gods are omnipotent, we don't blame them for not being able to subvert the cosmic order for our own comfort and rescue us from pain. We can, however, pray for their help and expect something to come around, because it is in the best interest of all parties concerned that everyone manages to do their sacred work with as much grace as possible.

Another huge question, at least for the followers of western polytheism, is: Why did our Gods allow the Christian holocaust to happen? Why allow thousands, and perhaps even millions, of people to be killed or forcibly converted to Christianity in fear of their lives? This is a question that has been asked by almost every serious converted student of Pagan theology I have observed. While there is no one answer, the various partial answers that we do have tend to underline many of the truths discussed in this book: that the Gods are not omnipotent, that they see things further and longer than we do ourselves, that they do not need us to exist, and that we humans do have a great deal of free will when it comes to our group relationship with them.

Let's start with that first one and speak it one more time, to drive it home: Our Gods are not omnipotent. They have the power to arrange synchronicity in this world, sometimes in amazing ways, in order to influence us to do what they want or believe is right. However, they must remain within their own laws and the limitations of their power. If any given human being is not "lawful prey" by cosmic standards, the Gods may not force them to do anything. They may ask, they may advise, they may keep suggesting, they may even arrange circumstances in such a way as to make their preferred road more easy and attractive and others less so, but if we absolutely refuse to move, then we will not move no matter what. We may suffer consequences later in the form of the returned energy of our decision and all the pain it caused, but we are always free, at least to some extent, to make our own mistakes. When thousands of people forswore their Gods and decided to join up with the new religion, they did so for their own reasons. Some were genuinely called, which happens. Many, perhaps, were less devoutly religious than we might like to conceive of them being, and converted for personal or political reasons that seemed more important to them than the love or wrath of vague beings that they did not expect to see or hear from. Some were driven by the damage that life had inflicted on them, a damage so loud and painful that no divine voice could penetrate it, and used religion as a convenient tool to express that pain and rage.

In the country of Iceland in the year 1000, the population was split between converted Christians and existing Pagans. The Christian population, eager to make Iceland an entirely Christian country—by force, if necessary, and with the encouragement of the violent and intolerant King Olaf of Norway—**informed the Pagan population that they would be slaughtered if they did not convert.** At that summer's Althing, Thorgeirr the Lawgiver was given the decision to decide whether the Pagans would fight back or convert. Thorgeirr was a devout Pagan, but he was known as a wise and fair man, so everyone agreed to abide by his decision.

To consult with the Gods on the matter, he "went under the cloak" for a day and a night, covering himself with a fur blanket without food or drink, praying for hours in the darkness. He emerged the next day and informed the people that the Gods had spoken: all Pagans were to convert, because there was no good way to win the war. The Christians were too many and they would all die, whereas if they lived and bent the knee to the Christian God, they would be able to quietly pass on their faith to future generations. Thorgeirr led the way by carrying his god-statues to a waterfall and flinging them over, and then knelt to be baptized. All of Iceland followed. If they had not, Snorri Sturluson might never have written his *Eddas*, and we would not have that knowledge today. One can only imagine the great love the Gods had for the people—**being willing to be abandoned by their worshipers rather than to see them all die.**

This story tells me that the Gods would rather see us live and convert than perish altogether, and it is likely that they saw the holocaust coming and understood its meaning. It is also likely that, in their long existence and longer reach of vision, that it would not have been nearly the hardship to wait for us to come around, unlike us and our short lives and views. Certainly they seem to be no worse for wear, now that more and more of us are giving them our attention. This reinforces the idea that they have lives beyond us. While our distance from them may cause our general connection to wane, that is less like their death and more like us merely cutting the phone line. When we rebuild it, they are still there and interested in connecting with us again.

Of course, it is not true that there will be no consequences for our actions. Some Pagan mystics aver that some, at least, of the ancestral Gods and spirits of European-descended people cursed their former followers when their ancient obligations were abandoned. This theory blames the generally spiritually unhealthy behavior of European-descended peoples for the last thousand years on this curse, and claims that it will only be lifted when there are enough converts to the Old Ways and the old obligations to make up for the numbers that were once lost—which, to be fair, is now only a small fraction of the European-descended people in the world.

However, there is also evidence that the Gods did not entirely abandon the world, but merely spoke to people—and accepted their offerings of various energies—through other means. Many Catholic saints are actually the names of Pagan God/desses with fictional stories slapped over them, and it is likely that they continued their work with us in that way. In addition, some people only converted in the very vaguest sense, and continued to respect some passed-down version of the old ways to one extent or another, without neighbors or clergy knowing about it. It takes far fewer people to create a divine connection than one might think.

Another theory that has been discussed by various mystics is the idea that the connection points—or perhaps one could say "soft spots" between our world and the various Otherworlds—are not always static with each other. This idea centers around the concept of cyclical orbits; that the Otherworlds, like the physical planets in our solar system, have their various cosmic "orbits" that bring them closer and further away from each other. Indeed, those mystics who have studied astrology and consider it to be not just some method of calculating probability and fate from the rocks that float around in our own dimension, but instead a way to calculate the Universal clock of cycles and synchronicity (of which those rocks happen to be only a paltry few markers), have intimated this possibility. As above, so below: all worlds have cyclical orbits of differing lengths, both in a physical sense and in a nonphysical sense. Just as the planets draw apart and together again, so do the Otherworlds. We can only see their conjunctions, as it were, to our world, but that doesn't mean that other connections are forming and drawing apart all the time.

If we take this concept as a given, then it is not a far stretch to assume that our psychic connections with the Gods might well wax and wane over the period of this cycle, which would manifest as various mass human choices—including, during a waning phase, the choice to forswear that connection entirely, and to turn instead to a deity whose Otherworld was drawing nearer. If the Otherworlds in question were to draw closer again, it would not be surprising for human beings to begin slowly to reconnect and turn to those older Gods once again. If we accept the idea that all things go in measured—and perhaps even measurable—cycles, then we can forgive our ancestors a great deal. We can also learn from what came before, and create future plans to hold on through another such period.

It might even be possible to clock those shifts via the astrological cosmic clock. We do know about the astrological "ages", roughly two-thousand-year periods that are "ruled by" (meaning strongly affected by the archetypes of) two opposing signs of the Zodiac, even if most of us only know about them through songs about the Age of Aquarius which is dawning now. We know that the dual archetypes of those signs echo throughout the "age" that they rule—for example, during the age of Cancer/Capricorn, the signs of Moon-Mother and Goat-Father, humanity's primitive art revolved around a mother-figure and a horned hunter-god. In the age of Gemini/Sagittarius, the signs of words and travel, we had the invention of alphabets and the mass migrations of the Indo-Europeans, among others. In the age of Taurus/Scorpio, signs concerned with gardening, stability, and death, we had the mass rise of agriculture-founded cities and funerary religions. During the age of Aries/Libra, signs representing war and justice, city-states and countries formed through law and martial aggression, and the Warrior and the Statesman were the prime divine archetypes. Then, two thousand years ago or thereabouts, we moved into the age of Pisces/Virgo, whose archetypes were the Sacrificial King and the Virgin. The rise of Christianity coincided with this era, and perhaps we can theorize that the Otherworld of those deities occupied the main cosmic connection for a time. Now, of course, we are entering into the age of Aquarius/Leo, whose main archetypes seem to be manifesting in—as an astrologer friend of mine pointed out—the Scientist and the Rock Star.

While it is doubtful that the astrological ages clock the connections of all Otherworlds—each unique connection may have its own astrologically-marked cycle of joining and parting with us—it may be possible, with work and observation of both ancient history and modern causality—to clock the cycles of our world's dance with various Otherworlds, and to have this as a tool to take action in future centuries. Who knows? Since what we know about the Gods—even after the entirety of this book is absorbed—is only a tiny fragment of what there is to understand, we may yet discover ways to predict and prevent humanity's slaughters in the name of their Gods. One thing is certain, however: Cosmic cycles may come and go, but we will never cease to explore and share the mysteries that the Gods hold out to us.

## About The Author

Raven Kaldera is a priest and minister of the First Kingdom Church of Asphodel, a Pagan church in Massachusetts, USA. He is also a Northern Tradition shaman, astrologer, diviner, and the author of too many books to list here. He gives workshops on various things Pagan, including theology, and loves his many, many Gods and spirits, all of them. He can be found at www.northernpaganism.org and www.ravenkaldera.org. 'Tis an ill wind that blows no minds.